Paris

by

LADURÉE

Paris

Chic City Guides

TEXT : Serge Gleizes

PHOTOGRAPHY : Pierre-Olivier Signe

VENDOME
SCRIPTUM

Paris is unique. A majestic, captivating capital. And it is here that the Ladurée story began and here that we have thrived since 1862. We love our city: its royal gardens, its Haussmannian façades, its boulevards and boutiques, its restaurants and riverside-walks along the shimmering Seine. Once upon a time Paris was but a small fortified town known as Lutetia, perched on a hill surrounded by water. Over the centuries the town grew, until it grandly became the world capital of the arts, haute couture, beauty, gastronomy, and decoration, and home to the finest museums and monuments in the world. It is also a city for strolling, amorous encounters and dreaming. It is impossible not to succumb to its charm.

It is here that our passion was born, and through our spirit and expertise we transformed our tearooms and boutiques into microcosms within the larger city, many located in historical locations such as the avenue des Champs-Élysées, rue Bonaparte, and rue Royale.

It is with great pleasure that we offer you this guide unveiling our secrets: our favourite haunts, the addresses of faithful friends and partners, and other quintessential purlieux we usually only share in a whisper. Precious places that make our city one of the most wonderful in the world!

We wish you a joyous journey through Paris *by* Ladurée!

LADURÉE *Paris*

Contents
page 142

Gourmandise

{ Gastronomy }

Grand restaurants, neighbourhood bistros, charming menus with traditional dishes, fusion cuisine with flavours of faraway lands: Paris has it all, gastronomy and eclecticism are *de rigueur*. Nestling in its streets are a whole host of family institutions, delicatessens, wine sellers, bakeries, chocolateries, and cheese mongers, the list is endless: proof that Paris is still the world capital of gastronomy. Ladurée shares this vision of our city and here are the addresses of our treasures, some well-known, others more uncharted, places where what is on the plate is as important as the atmosphere and welcome inside. Places where a love of good food is to be shared and celebrated!

The finest eateries in Paris. The restaurants, bars and bistros that dreams are made of. Their décors are exceptional, their menus scintillating, and their service impeccable. Here, dining is a privilege and a celebration in itself. The kind of place for which you have to dress your best.

⋯ LE GRAND VÉFOUR ⋯

Le Grand Véfour first opened in 1784 as the Café de Chartres, and was later frequented by Jean Cocteau, Jean Marais, Colette, Bérard and other stars of French cinema who adored its cuisine and *Second Empire* paintings. 1948 to 1984 saw the charismatic chef Raymond Oliver at the helm. In 2011, the Michelin-starred Guy Martin took over and, ever since, has been serving inventive traditional fare; of special note: their exquisite range of *gâteaux de Savoie*.

⁻ 17, rue de Beaujolais, 75001 Tel: 01 42 96 56 27 Metro: Palais-Royal
 www.grand-vefour.com

⋯ L'AMBROISIE ⋯

Don't expect ostentation or complicated cuisine at L'Ambroisie. For Bernard Pacaud and his son, Mathieu, authenticity is the *mot du jour*. Among the specialties are snail *parmentier* with wild garlic, a moka vacherin dessert with pearl meringues, and poached egg with a watercress sabayon served with green asparagus and caviar. A feast for the eyes and the tongue!

⁻ 9, place des Vosges, 75004 Tel: 01 42 78 51 45
 Metro: Chemin-Vert, Saint-Paul or Sully-Morland www.ambroisie-paris.com

⋯ THOUMIEUX ⋯

One of our favourite haunts for several reasons: firstly for its décor – produced by one of today's most high-profile interior architects, India Mahdavi; secondly, for the chef's famous menu of blue lobster, delicious cheeses, and a divine *île flottante*; finally, for the sophisticated finer details, such as the enchanting cutlery and porcelain. A perfect restaurant for intimate lunches or dinners.

⁻ 79, rue Saint-Dominique, 75007 Tel: 01 47 05 49 75
 Metro: Invalides or La Tour-Maubourg www.thoumieux.fr

... L'ARPÈGE ...

Here simplicity, authenticity and excellence combine to perfection, with a touch of humour, via the ersatz-bouquet table-decorations made of licorice sticks or ebony. Among the treasures from the kitchen: globe turnip sushi with a hint of geranium, lobster filets prepared in *Côte-du-Jura* wine, and a fresh *thermidrome* garlic *velouté*. Flavour for the mind, poetry on the plate, and beauty in the eye of the beholder.
– 84, rue de Varenne, 75007 Tel: 01 47 05 09 06 Metro: Varenne
   www.alain-passard.com

... LASSERRE ...

The open-roofed dining room on the first floor is a true delight and magnificent in summer. The menu is both classic and light, the artistry of Christophe Moret, from Alain Ducasse's Plaza Athénée, with Claire Heitzler providing desserts.
Two stars in the *Michelin guide*.
– 17, avenue Franklin-D.-Roosevelt, 75008 Tel: 01 43 59 02 13
   Metro: Franklin D. Roosevelt www.restaurant-lasserre.com

... LE CINQ ...

Le Cinq is the dining room at the Four Seasons Hôtel George V. With its grey and gold tones, 18th-century Franco-British furnishings and Regency mirrors, the two Michelin-starred restaurant exudes luxury. Christian Le Squer's fresh, creative fare is a fiesta of France's finest regional and seasonal products: expect *farandoles* of mushrooms, a delicate sea-bream and succulent Paris-Brest with Piedmont hazelnuts, among other wonders galore.
– 31, avenue George-V, 75008 Tel: 01 49 52 71 54 Metro: George V
   www.restaurant-lecinq.com

... LE JULES VERNE ...

On the second level of the Eiffel Tower is an elegant eatery designed by Patrick Jouin affording one of the most spectacular views of the capital. Run by Alain Ducasse and Pascal Féraud, it also offers gastronomic wonders to match the vista: duck *foie gras*, roast langoustine, sea bass *en meunière* and Mediterranean specialties.
– Tour Eiffel, 5, avenue Gustave-Eiffel (pilier sud), 75007 Tel: 01 45 55 61 44
   Metro: Dupleix www.lejulesverne-paris.com

Beside the Seine
¹ Le Voltaire

Le Voltaire is a typically Parisian brasserie ideally situated on the banks of the Seine and just around the corner to the charming rue du Bac, the musée d'Orsay and the Carré Rive Gauche – home to Paris's great antique dealers.

On the menu are exquisite fish and meat dishes: a delicious whiting *goujonnette* or their famous beef fillet with fries. A classic eatery and a favourite haunt of French movie stars.

⌐ 27, quai Voltaire, 75007
  Tel: 01 42 61 17 49, Metro: Rue du Bac

Heading South-West
² Le Basilic

A restaurant with a Basque-feel on the Sainte Clotilde basilica square. The Art Deco interior, leather banquettes, subdued lighting, antique mirrors and vintage posters bring a warm atmosphere, while the seasonal south-west French cuisine is simple and generous: leak vinaigrette, skate with capers, leg of lamb with fries, served with natural or organic wines – from the Basque region, *naturellement*!

⌐ 2, rue Casimir-Périer, 75007
  Tel: 01 44 18 94 64
  Metro: Solférino, Invalides,
  Assemblée nationale or Varenne
  www.restaurant-le-basilic.fr

Gastro-Bar
L'Atelier Saint-Germain de Joël Robuchon

Joël Robuchon's 'Ateliers' are essentially bar-restaurants, where you can dine at the bar and watch the kitchen at work. Chef Axel Mane's amazing menu features cult favourites such as black truffle with stewed potatoes and Colbert whiting.

The world-famous multi-Michelin-starred chef, Robuchon, entrusted the interior design to Pierre-Yves Rochon known for his palatial hotel interiors. The result: a forty-seat bar counter in a red and black theme.

There is another Atelier at l'Étoile. (Publicis Drugstore, 133, avenue des Champs-Élysées, 75008, Tel: 01 47 23 75 75).

⌐ Hôtel du Pont Royal,
  5, rue de Montalembert, 75007
  Tel: 01 42 22 56 56
  Metro: Rue du Bac
  www.atelier-robuchon-saint-germain.com

Flea Market Special!

¹ Ma Cocotte

One of the famous Clignancourt Flea Market's finest eateries. Its Philippe Starck décor has an original zingy feel: red brick walls, carpet mosaics and Droog Design toilets with sparkling white ceramic tiling.

Its simple, yet succulent food is a true pleasure: lentil salad, egg mayonnaise, rotisserie chicken, fish and chips, cheeseburgers, and for dessert a tantalizing toasted-almond rice pudding!

— 106, rue des Rosiers, 93400 Saint-Ouen
Tel: 01 49 51 70 00
Metro: Porte de Clignancourt
www.macocotte-lespuces.com

Design Décor

² Le Mama Shelter

A journey to this eatery on the east Parisian periphery may feel like an expedition, but it is definitely worthwhile. The Philippe Starck décor replete with vast bar, jukebox and wordplay on the ceiling, creates a distinctly trendy atmosphere, especially during fashion week.

Jérôme Banctel's menu, meanwhile, has a simple homely feel that is both droll and delicious: *parmentier* of duck confit, oven-baked macaroni with poached egg and Mostellos ham, roast smoked chicken, and for a succulent finale, a scrumptious rum-baba!

— 109, rue de Bagnolet, 75020
Tel: 01 43 48 48 48
Metro: Porte de Bagnolet or Gambetta
Other locations: www.mamashelter.com

Fish and Seafood

La Méditerranée

Created in 1942, La Méditerranée has never been so popular. It has both a prime location on one of the capital's finest squares, place de l'Odéon, overlooking the Odéon Théâtre de l'Europe; and an incredible fish and seafood menu – its speciality. Depending on the delivery, its oysters and urchins are among the best in Paris, not to mention the succulent honey-lacquered sea bass.

A perfect place to end the evening after a show in an elegant Mediterranean atmosphere, or a delicious starting point for a after-meal stroll in the Luxembourg gardens.

— 2, place de l'Odéon, 75006
Tel: 01 43 26 02 30, Metro: Odéon
www.la-mediterranee.com

Deliciously Retro

¹ Chez l'ami Louis

Behind the black façade and Vichy curtains you'll find a charming interior with a nostalgic feel: period tiles, vintage mouldings and 1950s bistro tables.

Louis Gadby's traditional cuisine features fine South-West classics: its speciality *foie gras*, and seasonal family fare.

⎯ 32, rue du Vertbois, 75003
   Tel: 01 48 87 77 48
   Metro: Temple

Warm and Traditional

² 'Chez Dumonet', restaurant Joséphine

Behind Chez Dumonet's attractive wood-clad exterior, Jean-Christian Dumonet offers traditional fare specializing in roasts, grilled meats, and cheese. Look out for their stuffed morello mushrooms, *foie gras* and the *soufflé* dessert.

Inside the tiled floors, dressers, etchings and engraved glasses make for a traditional homely bistro interior, where service is warm and refined, another feather in the cap of the restaurant's reputation.

⎯ 117, rue du Cherche-Midi, 75006
   Tel: 01 45 48 52 40
   Metro: Duroc or Falguière

South-West Wonders

³ La Fontaine de Mars

Renovated by its owners Christiane and Jacques Boudon in 2007, La Fontaine de Mars is one of the Paris's oldest bistros. The menu reflects the proprietors' south-western origins: delicious *foies gras*, duck *magrets* and *cassoulets*. The warm bistro interior replete with leather banquettes is cozy in winter, while in summer you can have lunch under the arcades on red-checked table-cloths and let yourself be lulled by the gentle whisper of the fountain where Napoleon's army once brought their horses to drink.

Leave room for dessert – the rum baba is irresistible! Open all year.

⎯ 129, rue Saint-Dominique, 75007
   Tel: 01 47 05 46 44
   Metro: École Militaire
   www.fontainedemars.com

Gourmet Bites
1 Shu

Shu's stone-wall and bare-beamed décor is as unusual as its menu, composed mainly of *kushikatsu* – intriguing deep-fried kebabs of meat, fish and vegetables in a fascinating range of tastes and textures, such as lotus root, *foie gras* and quail's egg served with a variety of sauces.

A delectable gourmet adventure.

— 8, rue Suger, 75006
Tel: 01 46 34 25 88
Metro: Saint-Michel or Odéon
www.restaurant-shu.com

In the Land of the Rising Sun
2 Yen

Not far from the Café de Flore, behind its Spartan façade, Yen serves delicious Japanese fare in a minimalist setting.

Here you'll find delicious prawn or vegetable tempura, hot or cold homemade *soba* buckwheat noodles served with sesame sauce, while for dessert, there is sesame or green tea ice cream to complete a delicious interlude in the Land of the Rising Sun.

A refreshing change from the usual sushi and sashimi menus available elsewhere.

— 22, rue Saint-Benoît, 75006
Tel: 01 45 44 11 18
Metro: Saint-Germain-des-Prés

Tokyo-Style Shopping

A handful of addresses to help you concoct your own umami-licious Japanese dishes at home: **Workshop Issé** (11, rue Saint Augustin, 75002; Tel: 01 42 96 26 74) – look out for its sakes, plum liqueurs, green teas, yuzu juices, Sansho peppers, and vinegars, etc., made by small, often legendary Japanese producers; **Kioko** (46, rue des Petits-Champs, 75002; Tel: 01 42 61 33 65), two floors offering a variety of rice, as well as seaweed, sauces, candies, fruits and organic Japanese vegetables; **Juji-ya** (46, rue Sainte-Anne, 75002; Tel: 01 42 86 02 22) a small boutique purveying bentos, those neat Japanese meal trays you compose yourself, to eat in or take away; **Kanae** (118, rue Lecourbe, 75015; Tel: 01 56 56 77 60), specialized in fresh exotic fruits, beers, sauces, and a frozen-food section.

Let's not forget the chicest Japanese range of all at **La Grande Épicerie de Paris** in Le Bon Marché (see page 26).

Art on a Plate

[1] Ze Kitchen Galerie

A homely eatery with a Zen feel. The fusion fare on offer reflects the chef and owner William Ledeuil's fascination with both French and Asian gastronomic traditions. Each dish is a miniature masterpiece of minimalist art in subtle flavours: roast langoustines with marinated citron and ginger, crab and coriander salad with finely sliced mango or kohlrabi, and rhubarb with a strawberry *fromage-blanc* sorbet.

The restaurant also stages contemporary art exhibitions.

⌐ 4, rue des Grands-Augustins, 75006
  Tel: 01 44 32 00 32
  Metro: Saint-Michel
  For their other address, visit:
  www.zekitchengalerie.fr

A Cocktail of Flavours

[2] Le Bar Ladurée

Fancy a change from the usual Ladurée style? Roxane Rodriguez's radiant décor provides the ideal backdrop for a multifarious menu catering for every moment of the day.

Breakfast? Freshly laid organic eggs, rose and raspberry French toast. Brunch? A carpaccio of organic sea bass with ginger, or a salmon piccata served with preserved lemons and oats, followed by Ispahan verrines and a Saint-Honoré gateau, bringing fresh twists to French classics. For lunch and beyond? Michel Lerouet's menu of blinis, seasonal salads and divine slices of salmon.

⌐ 13, rue Lincoln, 75008
  Tel: 01 40 75 08 75
  Metro: George V
  www.laduree.fr

Macaron Cocktails

Ladurée's guiding light is naturally the *macaron*, and our rue Lincoln bar is proud of its unique *macaron*-inspired cocktails served with their accompanying patisserie: *Caramel à la fleur de sel* (vodka, Giffard caramel liqueur, toffee nut syrup, caramel crème); Pistachio (vodka, ginger liqueur, pistachio syrup and crème); Rose (vodka, rose juice, rose syrup and crème); Lemon, Coffee, Raspberry, Orange Blossom, and Vanilla *macaron* cocktails, among many others. These delicious heady concoctions are ideal as late-afternoon aperitifs to settle the senses, ease the mind and set your taste buds tingling.

Haute Couture

¹ Emporio Armani Caffè

In the heart of Saint-Germain-des-Prés opposite the Deux Magots, you'll find a swanky black façade housing a *café-brasserie* and fashion-boutique, where chic is the name of the game. The chef Massimo Mori offers delicious *burrata, tortelli veneziani* or *vitello tonnato* (slithers of roast veal served with a tuna and caper sauce) accompanied by excellent wines and an enticing coffee ice cream for dessert.

3pm-8pm, don't miss the 'Armani afternoons': ice creams made to order served with an espresso, *meringues* and caramelized hazelnuts.

— 149, boulevard Saint-Germain, 75006
Tel: 01 45 48 62 15
Metro: Saint-Germain-des-Prés
For other address, visit:
www.massimomori.net

Southern Cuisine

² Le Perron

A well-kept Left Bank secret offering the finest in Southern Italian food from Sicily, Sardinia and Abruzzo. The antipasti, pasta, fried artichokes, langoustine tagliatelle, and asparagus or saffron *risotto* are 'Bellisima!', as is the wine menu.

The setting is friendly and unobtrusive: bare-stone walls and wooden beams, bistro banquettes and white table cloths, an ideal departure point for a delicious journey in flavour.

— 6, rue Perronet, 75007
Tel: 01 45 44 71 51
Metro: Saint-Germain-des-Prés
or Rue du Bac
www.restaurantleperron.fr

Transalpine Tastes

³ Pizza chic

As the name suggests, Pizza Chic offers pizzas in a chic, cozy and warm, yet minimalist setting with broad bay windows, white tablecloths and silver cutlery. The fine-crust pizzas prepared before your eyes are generously topped and its Italian wine list is lush. For desserts choose the *sgroppino*, a Venetian speciality of lemon sorbet, *grappa*, *prosecco* and *limoncello*.

A stone's throw from the Luxembourg gardens, Pizza Chic is the 6th-arrondissement's most glamorous pizzeria!

— 13, rue de Mézières, 75006
Tel: 01 45 48 30 38
Metro: Saint-Sulpice
www.pizzachic.fr

View over the Louvre
¹ Le Café Marly

Designed by Olivier Gagnère and Yves Taralon, Le Café Marly offers a choice of fantastic vistas: inside overlooks one of the Louvre's famous sculpture galleries, while outside, the arcade terrace affords a view of its courtyard and Pei's famous pyramid.

Among its dishes are organic salmon and the 'Crying Tiger' created by the renowned Thai chef, Thiou.

Ideal for a business lunch, a romantic *tête-à-tête* or a quiet drink watching the sunset caress the Arc de Triomphe du Carrousel.

⌐ 93, rue de Rivoli, 75001
Tel: 01 49 26 06 60
Metro: Palais-Royal
www.beaumarly.com

Flea Market Special
² Les Gastropodes

A stylish micro-bistro composed of a single counter and a handful of tables. Here the chefs take care of service and their menu is mouthwatering: burgers with *remoulade*, crispy fish and chips, pastrami sandwiches, salted butter caramel ice-cream and the snail *brioche* with mustard sprouts and blackberries – a tongue-in-cheek reference to the bistro's gastropod moniker.

⌐ 132-140, rue des Rosiers,
93400 Saint-Ouen
Tel: 06 82 66 05 34
Metro: Porte de Clignancourt

Among the Literati
³ Les Deux Magots

The Saint Germain des Prés made famous by Picasso, Sartre, James Joyce and the young Ernest Hemingway. The décor is unique and the waiter service exceptional; the menu is equally appealing: excellent steak *tartare*, crisp tender fries and a traditional to-die-for hot chocolate served with melting squares of dark chocolate.

At the witching hour, the Saint Germain des Prés church opposite grows dark which means: the time has come for a *campari*!

⌐ 6, place Saint-Germain-des-Prés, 75006
Tel: 01 45 48 55 25
Metro: Saint-Germain-des-Prés
www.lesdeuxmagots.fr

The History Bar
La Palette

A survivor of the Bohemian period, this legendary bistro with its elegant façade and dining room decorated in 1930s–1940s ceramics and paintings is a listed historical building. Among the house specialties are organic eggs, locally-sourced farm cheeses and Alverta caviar from Petrossian. If food is not your fancy, feel free to take a drink on the terrace and watch the world going by on the attractive rue Jacques-Callot.

⌐ 43, rue de Seine, 75006
Tel: 01 43 26 68 15
Metro: Mabillon or Odéon
www.cafelapaletteparis.com

A Mouthful of Hospitality

¹ Le Pain quotidien

One of the first boulangerie-patisserie-tea rooms to have adopted the *table d'hôte* (common table) principle. The setting is redolent of traditional houses of yore: high ceilings, stone walls, glass roof and honey teak shelves bearing jars of honey, oil, preserves and other spreadable delights.

The menu is *à la mode*: detox salad, organic soup of the day, and vegetarian hotpot; for dessert, waffles with confectioners' sugar and chocolate *bombe*. You can even buy bread, sandwiches and *viennoiseries* to take away.

⌐ 25, rue de Varenne, 75007
Tel: 01 45 44 02 10
Metro: Sèvres-Babylone
or Rue du Bac
For other addresses, visit:
www.lepainquotidien.com

Seasonal Treats

² Cojean

The capital's trendiest self-service canteen, replete with high-stools and large bay windows. Pick up a metal basket and fill it with whatever you fancy: pots of lemon, thyme and zucchini soup, prawn *risotto* with green curry or white pineapple salad – to eat-in or take-away.

The meals are fresh and wholesome, balanced and delicious, crammed with seasonal products and surprise packages such as tapioca pearls, an array of fruit delights and *bubble tea* – a Taiwanese speciality. The personnel are delightful and the fetching sky-blue t-shirt uniform puts a sparkle in their eyes.

⌐ 42, boulevard Raspail, 75007
Tel: 01 45 48 98 87
Metro: Sèvres-Babylone
For other addresses, visit: www.cojean.fr

A Hint of Britain

The Hôtel Raphael bar

The soft lighting, antique wooden panelling and red velvet armchairs make the Hôtel Raphael bar one of the smartest English bars in the capital. With its quick lunch menu, the hotel is also a haven of peace and quiet amidst the bustling city.

The hotel meanwhile has terraces overlooking the Eiffel Tower, boasts the finest all-pristine-white suite in Paris and in the past has played host to a smorgasbord of French stars: the singer Serge Gainsbourg, the actress Arielle Dombasle and the writer Bernard-Henri Lévy, to name but a few.

⌐ 17, avenue Kléber, 75016
Tel: 01 53 64 32 00
Metro: Kléber
www.raphael-hotel.com

The Premiere Supermarket

[1] La Grande Épicerie de Paris

Le Bon Marché, opened its food department in 1923 and became in 1978 La Grande Épicerie de Paris, the *nec plus ultra* of Paris groceries. Today, under the guidance of Jean-Jacques Massé, it also purveys delicious homemade bread, desserts and more. The grandest grocery in the Parisian 'hood.

– 38, rue de Sèvres, 75007
 Tel: 01 44 39 81 00
 Metro: Sèvres-Babylone
 www.lagrandeepicerie.com

Exceptional Condiments

[2] Entrepôt Épices Roellinger

Michelin-starred chef, Olivier Roellinger is based in Cancale on the north coast of France and is famous for his incredible menus and his spice and condiment collections. Each colourful jar of spices, peppers, grains and vanillas exudes heady aromas that will send you journeying to faraway lands. There are also oils, orange and cinnamon salted-butter cookies, and the incredible *Rêves d'étoiles* spice infusion for cold winter nights.

– 51 bis, rue Sainte-Anne, 75002
 Tel: 01 42 60 46 88
 Metro: Pyramides or Quatre-Septembre
 www.epices-roellinger.com

Farm Flavours

[3] It Mylk

The Lorenzi sisters developed their own concept based on fresh seasonal products and internet sales offering a luscious range of dairy produce and delicious milkshakes (strawberry, raspberry, praline or cocoa) using organic milk from Viltain farm cows.

Their 0%-fat cheesecakes and frozen yoghurts met with huge success in New York and Tokyo, and recently It Mylk has launched its first range of 0%-fat farmhouse yoghurts with an agave syrup.

– 1, place Jane-Évrard, 75016 and 6th floor of the Galeries Lafayette,
 48, boulevard Haussmann, 75009
 Metro: La Muette or Havre-Caumartin
 For other address, visit: www.itmylk.fr

A Scent of Spice

Izraël

An incredible spice-laden exotic grocery in the heart of Paris, a caravanserai of wonders from faraway lands. There's Turkish Delight, rose water, orange blossom water, dried and candied fruit, olives, cashew nuts, saffron, peppers and spices, amid a décor of flour sacks, dried chili peppers hanging from the ceiling, and shelves crammed with biscuits. Let your mind wander, let your taste buds dream.

– 30, rue François-Miron, 75004
 Tel: 01 42 72 66 23
 Metro: Hôtel de Ville or Saint-Paul

A Walk on the Organic Side

[1] L'Épicerie générale

Enticing cream storefront, sagging white shelves, white walls and teak furniture, a small, simple old-school grocery promoting everything wonderful in France: small producers, natural organic products and the pleasure of sharing. L'Épicerie générale offers *charcuterie*, wines, wholegrain loaves, spices, fruit, olive oil, jams, Hennequin Ile d'Yeu conserves, and a range of excellent organic sandwiches.

Among its more unusual products are Miel Béton from the nearby cement-capital of France, Saint-Denis, candles exuding fragrances of the undergrowth, and an organic vodka distilled in the town of Cognac. The store's owl logo is especially cute.

- 43, rue de Verneuil, 75007
  Tel: 01 42 60 51 78
  Metro: Solférino
  For another address, visit:
  www.epiceriegenerale.fr

Treasures of the Mediterranean

[2] Da Rosa

José Da Rosa has traveled the length and breadth of Spain, Italy and Portugal to bring back the finest of foods expressing an undying respect for Mother Nature. Among his *habitués'* favourites are *Bellota* ham, *lardo di Colonnata*, tuna belly, olive oil, white *tarama*, and a collection of rare and herbal teas. The store's reputation initially spread by word-of-mouth and now France's finest chefs visit in search of that special exotic touch to lend their cuisine that extra *je ne sais quoi*.

If you want to drum up a last-minute aperitif with tapas and other world-food specialties, this is your place.

- 62, rue de Seine, 75006
  Tel: 01 40 51 00 09
  Metro: Mabillon
  For other addresses, visit: www.darosa.fr

Bella Italia

[3] Coopérative Latte Cisternino

The best of Italy's regional farm cooperatives, where products are delivered fresh from their producers every Thursday. Walls covered in postcards, shelves sagging beneath the weight of creamy *Puglia burratas*, ricottas, fresh pasta, pizza dough, *Parma* hams, and *mozzarella di bufala*. The store attracts tourists and Italian ex-pats homesick for authentic flavours.

You'll find two other Latte Cisternino stores at 108, rue Saint-Maur, 75011, and 37, rue Godot-de-Mauroy, 75009.

- 17, rue Geoffroy-Saint-Hilaire, 75005
  Tel: 01 83 56 90 67
  Metro: Censier-Daubenton or Saint-Marcel

Regional Ambrosia

1 Legrand Filles and Fils

Created by Lucien Legrand during the 1976 heatwave, the interior décor – mosaic floors, cork marquetry ceiling, brass-clad windows and varnished counters – provides the perfect backdrop for an olfactory-overload of wines, coffees and teas.

Legrand is simultaneously a wine merchant, delicatessen, library, tasting counter and lounge looking out onto the gorgeous Galerie Vivienne. Delicious nectars are served all day with toast with Baltic salmon or *terrines* from Hardouin.

– 1, rue de la Banque, 75002
Tel: 01 42 60 07 12
Metro: Sentier or Pyramides
www.caves-legrand.com

The Pleasures of the Vine

2 La Cave de Joël Robuchon

Joël Robuchon is the world's foremost Michelin-starred chef. But a stone's throw away, you'll find his Atelier restaurant, popular for its excellent bar menu. This is his wine cellar, a delectably chic black interior subtly lit by red presentation alcoves, a haven to exquisite wines and *armagnacs* with customized labels.

If you don't have the time to visit La Cave in Paris, you'll also find Joël Robuchon's wine cellars in Beirut and Tokyo.

– 3, rue Paul-Louis-Courier, 75007
Tel: 01 42 22 11 02
Metro: Rue du Bac
www.joel-robuchon.net

Precious Nectars

Maison Ryst-Dupeyron

Step beyond one of rue du Bac's most attractive wood-panelled façades, and you'll find shelves laden with precious wines and spirits.

Founded in 1905, the Maison Ryst-Dupeyron specializes in brandies exuding aromas of prunes, vanilla and other heady concoctions reputed for their long oak barrel maturation. There are also white and Tawny ports – some organic, classic and vintage *armagnacs*, Speyside and Highland whiskys, Dupeyron wines, bordeaux *grands crus* and other marvels such as prune-cream chocolates.

– 79, rue du Bac, 75007
Tél: 01 45 48 80 93
Metro: Rue du Bac
www.maisonrystdupeyron.com

CAVIAR D'IRAN

CAVIAR DE RUSSIE

SAUMON SAUVAGE
DE NORVEGE

SAUMON BALTIQUE
BLANC

SAUMON ECOSSAIS

CRABE ROYAL

ANGUILLE FINE
DANOISE

$\frac{1}{1}\Big|\frac{1}{1}$

Black Gold

[1] Caviar Kaspia

Honey teak panelling, displays of fine porcelain, and antique paintings on the walls: Caviar Kaspia is one of the most elegant Russian restaurants in Paris, a chic and cozy haven of tranquillity, perfect for some downtime while perusing the district's sublime department stores.

Savour poached eggs and caviar, salmon roe, blinis, oven-grilled Vladivostok potatoes and vodka-babas for dessert. Simple authentic dishes that beautifully express their scrumptious ingredients.

- 17, place de la Madeleine, 75008
  Tel: 01 42 65 33 32
  Metro: Madeleine
  For another address, visit:
  www.kaspia.fr

Treasures of the Sea

Caviar Petrossian

If you're looking for caviar, then Petrossian is your place. Naturally there is fine, classic and cream caviar in all its forms, but also other maritime marvels such as smoked salmon, sea urchin roe, king crab tarama, Russian-style smoked sprat filets, anchovies with chili, and fish soup – delicacies that will turn any brunch, lunch or dinner into a gourmet feast.

Created by the Melkoum brothers and Mouchegh Petrossian in 1920, this world-renowned establishment also offers teas, *foie gras*, brandies, liqueurs and their delicious chocolate- vodka pearls.

- 18, boulevard de La Tour-Maubourg, 75007
  Tel: 01 44 11 32 22
  Metro: La Tour-Maubourg
  For other addresses,
  visit: www.petrossian.fr

◆◆◆

French Caviar

Once upon a time, caviar was the exclusive preserve of Russia, Iran and the Caspian Sea. Today sturgeons' egg caviar harvested in many far-flung cold-water corners of France and Ireland is also excellent. Created in 1997, **the Comptoir du caviar** (Tel: 01 34 97 21 21) has a production unit in Mulcent, in the Yvelines, producing caviar, but also salmon and trout roe, tarama, and sea urchin and lumpfish roe; **Sturia** based in Saint-Sulpice-and-Cameyrac, near Bordeaux (Tel: 05 57 34 45 40) is the leading French producer of sturgeon's caviar; **Caviar de France** in Biganos in the Gironde region (Tel: 05 56 82 64 42) is known for its exceptional environment and its crystalline waters; **Caviar perle noire** (Tel: 05 53 29 68 13) is made in Eyzies in the northern Périgord.

Sweet Reliquary

[1] Pâtisserie des Tuileries

Life's Little Weaknesses

[2] La Pâtisserie des rêves

Sébastien Gaudard had a dream, a dream of traditional French pastries such as the Saint-Honoré, Paris-Brest, Othello, rum baba, lemon and pear tart and Black Forest cake. But he wanted something different, so he created a new concept, a minimalist shrine to pastry where his miracles are presented beneath glass cloches like relics.

Alongside his marvels of pastry you'll find delicious ice creams and chocolates, while his seasonal Christmas creations are divine.

⌐ 1, rue des Pyramides, 75001
  Tel: 01 71 18 24 70
  Metro: Palais-Royal
  For another address, visit:
  www.sebastiengaudard.com

A vibrant candy store setting with gentle lighting and vibrant colours where pastries are presented under glass cloches as in times of yore. The concept is as exquisite as the pastries. We are particularly fond of its *Grand Cru*, a marvel that is 100%-chocolate, its Paris-Brest, its vanilla *millefeuille*, its puff-pastry *brioches*, and seasonal *gâteaux* such as their orange or strawberry tarts.

The god of these small miracles is Philippe Conticini, who has also written a recipe book of Nutella-based desserts.

⌐ 93, rue du Bac, 75007
  Tel: 01 42 84 00 82
  Metro: Rue du Bac or Sèvres-Babylone
  For other addresses, visit:
  www.lapatisseriedesreves.com

Haute Couture Patisseries

Today's leading patisserie chefs working the world's palaces and grand restaurants have been falling over each other to open their own chocolate and pastries outlets.
There are Sébastien Gaudard and Philippe Conticini, but also Alain Ducasse with **La Manufacture de chocolat** (see page 37), Jean-François Piège with **Gâteaux Thoumieux**, Hugues Pouget with **Hugo & Victor**, Christophe Adam, creator of **L'Éclair de génie**, Cyril Lignac with **La Patisserie Cyril Lignac**, Manuel Martinez with **La Maison du chou**, Christophe Michalak with **Michalak Take-Away**. All boutiques offer the chance to succumb to the lure of exquisite pastries and confections without having to venture into the sometimes more foreboding atmospheres of grand hotels or Michelin-starred restaurants.

Fine-Crafted Flavours

[1] Manufacture Alain Ducasse

Housed in a former workshop, the boutique near Bastille is an attractive combination of brickwork, curvaceous glass counters, industrial lamps and old-school machinery, a reminder of bygone days when the district was a hub of manufactories. Today the spanners and hammers have been replaced by chocolate bars, *ganaches*, heavenly bite-sized morsels of intense cocoa-bean pleasure and chocolate spreads galore. Look out for the famous *Mendiant* crammed with dried and candied fruit, and *Roc*, bite-sized marvels of crisped cereals and candied fruit covered in divine dark chocolate.

These are just a few of the splendours dispensed by Alain Ducasse and his chocolate-master general, Nicolas Berge.

– 40, rue de la Roquette, 75011
Tel: 01 48 05 82 86
Metro: Bastille or Bréguet-Sabin
www.lechocolat-alainducasse.com

Mad about Chocolate

[2] Les Marquis de Ladurée

Welcome to another of our epicurean arcadia. First there is our trademark Ladurée décor, an urbane nod to the aesthetic codes of the 18th-century nobility, then there is our sophisticated range of chocolate marvels, created by Julien Christophe and pastry-chef Yann Mengui: chocolate and coconut *religieuses marquises*, *camées*, chocolate *macarons*, chocolate bars and gingerbread – even the selection boxes are collector's items.

Warning: do not miss the *viennoiseries*, the yuzu chocolate Saint-Honoré, the magnificent total chocolate tart and the *religieuse marquise* passion.

– 14, rue de Castiglione, 75001
Tel: 01 42 60 86 92
Metro: Tuileries or Pyramides
www.laduree.com

Fruit and Candy

Boissier

Boissier is Paris's temple to traditional candy. Once upon a time, the sweet-toothed Parisian hankering for a sugar-kick could step from his carriage and spirit away elegant boxes of confectionery – fruit drops of every hue: cherry, raspberry, pear, or apricot. The same is true today, with the added addition of a phenomenal range of chocolate, including chocolate petals scented with rose, violet, verbena, lavender, and jasmine.

You'll also find accompaniments such as preserves, teas and candied chestnuts.

– 184, avenue Victor-Hugo, 75116
Tel: 01 45 03 50 77
Metro: Rue de la Pompe
For other outlets, visit:
www.maison-boissier.com

The Land of Herbs

[1] L'Herboristerie du Palais-Royal

Set in the Palais Royal, L'Herboristerie's stone-clad façade conceals honey teak shelving sagging with dried herbs, herbal infusions, and vegetable extracts, as well as natural cosmetics, recipe books and health and gardening manuals. Here you'll find every plant from Mother Nature's generous garden from angelica and verbena, to chervil, St. John's Wort and elderflower.

Of particular note: their Palais-Royal blends, the rosebud infusion – and the attractive Kraft paper packaging and labels add an attractive bonus.

- 11, rue des Petits-Champs, 75001
  Tel: 01 42 97 54 68
  Metro: Bourse or Pyramides
  www.herboristerie.com

Welcome to Seedland

[2] La Pistacherie

A boutique oozing sophistication that is redolent of late 19th-century apothecaries and which dispenses wholesome sustenance for the body and soul. This is the home of dried fruits, berries and nuts: pistachios from Central Asia and macadamias from Australia, cranberries from Canada and Goji berries from Tibet, all presented in glass presentation cases or concealed in thermally-controlled drawers to conserve their powers.

There are two wonderful boutiques to discover – rue Rambuteau and place de l'Alma.

- 67, rue Rambuteau, 75004,
  and 5, place de l'Alma, 75008
  Tel: 01 42 78 84 55 and 01 44 43 03 26
  Metro: Rambuteau and Alma-Marceau
  www.lapistacherie.eu

The Paris Tea Party

[3] Mariage frères

Colonial counters, exotic furniture and metal tea-tins lining the walls, and vendors in immaculate, starched linen uniforms: Mariage frères has been purveying the world's finest teas since 1854 and have always remained faithful to the traditional tea emporium setting. Each time a tea-tin is opened rich, vibrant aromas fill the air; visiting Mariage frères is an education in tea itself.

Apart from their famous formidable blends, they also sell gift cases, incense, perfumed candles, jellies, cookies and chocolates.

The Left-Bank tearoom has a meal menu with salmon in matcha tea or smoked duck *magret* with Jade Mountain tea. You'll find other emporiums near Étoile, the Louvre and in the Marais.

- 13, rue des Grands-Augustins, 75006
  Tel: 01 40 51 82 50
  Metro: Saint-Michel
  For other addresses, visit:
  www.mariagefreres.com

Cheesy Passions
¹ Barthélemy

A tiny, old-school cheese-monger with traditional façade, mosaic floor, and marble counter, run by a professional cheese-maker, Nicole Barthélemy. The store offers the finest of France's farmhouse varieties such as *Saint Nectaire, Cantal, Reblochon, Camembert, Brie,* and *Saint-Marcellin.* Not forgetting Barthélemy's famous 'Fontainebleau', a savoury, airy, chantilly-whipped *fromage blanc* – dairy paradise indeed!

Incidentally, Barthélemy is also the official supplier to the President and the government.

– 51, rue de Grenelle, 75007
  Tel: 01 42 22 82 24
  Metro: Rue du Bac

Yesterday's Bread!
² Boulangerie Paul

Founded 125 years ago in Lille, Paul is more than a traditional *boulangerie*; it is also a successful concept firmly founded on the values of the past. Here you'll find the tastes and textures of yesteryear from its traditional loaves – walnut, wholegrain, pretzels and badines – to its *patisseries, viennoiseries*, hot ready-made meals, salads and delicious sandwiches to eat-in or take-away.

The owner Francis Holder is a passionate perfectionist who pays meticulous attention to every detail from the trademark black façades to vintage furniture.

– 35, rue Tronchet, 75008
  and 17 and 21, rue de Buci, 75006
  Tel: 01 40 17 99 54 and 01 55 42 02 23
  Metro: Havre-Caumartin and Odéon
  For other addresses, visit: www.paul.fr

Cheese Bars

Across Paris is a range of warm and friendly bars dedicated to the tasting of the latest cheese-sensations: **Androuet** (37, rue de Verneuil, 75007, Tel: 01 42 61 97 55), which has a reputation in England and Sweden; **La Coop** (9, rue Corneille, 75006; Tel: 01 43 29 91 07), a vaulted cellar near the Luxembourg Gardens, belonging to the Beaufortain cooperative dairy; **Fil'O' Fromage** (12, rue Neuve-Tolbiac, 75013; Tel: 01 53 79 13 35), look out for names like Munster, Saint Sauveur, Agour, and Roquefort – rich pungent French cheeses of the like you'll only find here; **L'Affineur affiné** (51, rue Notre-Dame-de-Lorette, 75009; Tel: 09 66 94 22 15), known for its cheese-based lunch menus served with fruit jellies and preserves; **Mozza & Co** is a roving trattoria-truck often to be found 11, quai Anatole-France, which is worth tracking down for its deliciously creamy mozzarella (Tel: 06 50 02 50 53).

Mode & Beauté
{ Fashion & Beauty }

Haute couture, prêt-à-porter from France and abroad, vintage stores purveying haute couture at affordable prices, lingerie boutiques, accessories, gloves, shoes, and jewellery stores dispensing vintage and costume jewellery. Paris is not only the gourmet centre of the planet it is also the world's fashion capital. Certain streets and boulevards – Avenue Montaigne, rue du Faubourg Saint-Honoré, rue de Grenelle, boulevard Saint-Germain – are wonderlands of global renown. This guide offers an elite selection of the finest beauty salons and perfumeries, dispensing exquisite beauty care and unique fragrances. Savour our journey through Paris's finest emporiums of luxury and aesthetics.

The essentials

Prada, Christian Dior, Lanvin, Hermes, Chanel, and Louis Vuitton: globally renowned institutions purveying not only the haute couture of which dreams are made, but also prêt-à-porter and those chic yet affordable fundamentals that accessorize those dreams.

... PRADA ...

Prada is both a designer label and a mindset, a style. It's not just the 'closet-essential-little-black-number', but also three-quarter-length coats, flared skirts, skinny pants and cashmere twin-sets, as well as pumps, bags, sunglasses and jewellery, all part of the cherished arsenal of today's *femme à la mode*. Each boutique is also an architectural masterpiece.

− 10, avenue Montaigne 75008 🖎 Tel: 01 53 23 99 40 🖎 Metro: Franklin D. Roosevelt
🖎 For other addresses, visit: www.prada.com

... CHRISTIAN DIOR ...

Since Christian Dior opened in 1946, the label has been the emblem of French haute couture. Alongside the white and grey showroom and its famous Louis XVI medallion furnishings is the perfumery, a curiosity cabinet dispensing their famous private collection of Colognes.

− 30, avenue Montaigne, 75008 🖎 Tel: 01 40 73 73 73 🖎 Metro: Franklin D. Roosevelt,
🖎 For other addresses, visit: www.dior.com

... LANVIN ...

Lanvin offers the haute couture of prêt-à-porter: refined evening dresses, drape-necks, furs and accessories, and their unique style is reflected in their tongue-in-cheek window displays. After the designer Alber Elbaz, Lucas Ossendrijver took over at the helm. Today Lanvin is one of the world's most desirable labels.

− 15 and 22, rue du Faubourg-Saint-Honoré, 75008 🖎 Tel: 01 44 71 33 33
🖎 Metro: Madeleine 🖎 www.lanvin.com

... HERMÈS ...

The famous temple of silk scarves, Kelly bags, heavenly Hermessence perfumes, jewellery and a whole department dedicated to the home. Their spectacular 6th arrondissement boutique is housed in a former swimming pool and its windows displays extol the wonders of the 'Petit h' collection launched by the decorative arts icon, Pascale Mussard. The 'Petit h' concept? To create lamps, teapots, dressers, jewellery, screens and stationery using cast-offs from Hermès' own workshops. The result? Poetry in lifestyle.

‒ 24, rue du Faubourg-Saint-Honoré, 75008, and 17, rue de Sèvres, 75006
  Tel: 01 40 17 46 00 and 01 42 22 80 83 Metro: Madeleine and Sèvres-Babylone
  For other addresses, visit: www.hermes.fr

... CHANEL ...

Now under the guidance of Karl Lagerfeld and his distinctive panache, Chanel is an essential for its classic suits and contemporary prêt-à-porter, cashmere twin-sets, make-up and perfumes – like the legendary Numero 5 adored by Marylin Monroe. It is also an essential visit for a glimpse of the mirrored staircase where Norma Jeane's stilettoed swagger was once a familiar sight.

‒ 31, rue Cambon, 75001 Tel: 01 44 50 70 00 Metro: Madeleine
  For other addresses, visit: www.chanel.fr

... LOUIS VUITTON ...

To complement their Champs-Élysées flagship, the showcase to their emblematic monogrammed luggage range, LV opened an exclusive boutique in Saint-Germain-des-Prés specializing in luggage, fashion, office accessories and stationery. It matters not if it's fifty-dollar scarves or a twenty-thousand-dollar trunks that set your eyes aglow; customers all receive the same treatment and vendors are never selective about whom they serve. *Au contraire*, they are only too happy to provide you with coffee before settling down to unveil LV's myriad treasures, whether you're buying or not. Style incarnate!

‒ 6, place Saint-Germain-des-Prés, 75006 Tel: 01 45 49 62 32
  Metro: Saint-Germain-des-Prés For other addresses, visit: www.louisvuitton.fr

Second Skin

[1] Azzedine Alaïa

The 1980s' most emblematic designer, Azzedine Alaïa, was a hardcore proponent of hand-stitched and made-to-measure. Back then, he created a unique style that fashion followed; today he's moved on to haute couture. Alaïa is the king of silhouette perfection. His dresses are so impeccably cut, they hug the body like a second skin.

In the heart of the Marais, on the corner of rue de Moussy and rue de la Verrerie, his gigantic showroom was decorated by the American painter and filmmaker Julian Schnabel. Here Alaïa's collections find pride of place alongside exhibitions of contemporary art.

– 18, rue de la Verrerie, 75004
Tel: 01 42 72 19 19
Metro: Saint-Paul
For another address, visit: www.alaia.fr

An Eclectic Concept Store

[2] L'Éclaireur

An Aladdin's cave of fashion, where collections by Alexander McQueen, Alexandra Wagner, Anne Valérie Hash, Balenciaga, Carven, Céline, and Dries Van Noten cohabit with interior décor by Piero Fornasetti, perfume by Frédéric Malle, jewellery by Rosa Maria and San Lorenzo, and pieces from Pascale Mussard's 'Petit h' limited series collection.

France's first concept store was the brainchild of Armand and Martine Hadida and opened in 1980; you'll find their other boutique between rue Royale, home to the finest tableware establishments of Paris, and rue du Faubourg-Saint-Honoré, home to famous luxury prêt-à-porter labels.

– 18, rue Boissy-d'Anglas, 75008
Tel: 01 53 43 03 70
Metro: Concorde
For other addresses, visit:
www.leclaireur.com

Colour and Sex

Marni

Created in 1994 by Consuelo Castiglioni, Marni is a distinctly contemporary Italian brand purveying clothing, bags and jewellery, perfect for the elegant modern female physique, in a selection of prints, luxurious materials, impeccable finishes, asymmetrical feminine cuts, and exquisitely subtle greens, ochres, blues and reds.

The boutique's architecture is magnificent and its décor chic and sophisticated; the collections are hung spaciously on wall rails, improving visibility, an attractive quirk of presentation.

– 57, avenue Montaigne, 75008
Tel: 01 56 88 08 08
Metro: Franklin D. Roosevelt
www.marni.com

Printed Paradise

Pucci

The famous 1950s pop label with its famous pop prints and geometric motifs. We have a special fondness for the scarves, ski suits, Moon Boots, ultra-bright prints, psychedelic colours and stretch fabrics.

Created in 1947 by the Marchese di Barsento, Emilio Pucci, the prince of printed fabrics, the establishment is a seventh heaven of grace, glamour and sensuality in keeping with its Florentine origins. Today the label's adventures in pop allure continue under Peter Dundas.

— 46-48, avenue Montaigne, 75008
Tel: 01 47 20 04 45
Metro: Franklin D. Roosevelt
www.emiliopucci.com

The Queen of the Wrap Dress

Diane von Fürstenberg

This attractive 8th-arrondissement boutique is perfect for unearthing that simple waist-hugging printed jersey wrap-dress. At Ladurée, we are also big fans of their skirts, blouses and tunics printed with floral, geometrical 1970s motifs.

Having become famous for her legendary wrap dress, Diane von Fürstenberg debuted in prêt-à-porter in 1974, creating collections with bright colours and sensual lines.

Her slogan, 'Feel like a woman. Wear a dress' still holds true today. Meanwhile we mustn't forget her eminently chic shoes, bags, scarves and sunglasses.

— 29, rue François-Ier, 75008
Tel: 01 40 70 00 90
Metro: Franklin D. Roosevelt
For another address, visit: www.dvf.com

Extravagance and Elegance

[1] Paul Smith

Paris loves Paul Smith for its elegant men's suits with sophisticated lines and red silk linings, floral shirts, striped socks and exquisitely comfortable British shoes. We also love his madcap window displays.

Above all, the eclectic Mr Smith has turned kitsch and extravagance into a subtle art form. Having branched out beyond his legendary stripes, he now deals in décor and has even opened an antiques gallery on Albemarle Street in London.

— 22, boulevard Raspail, 75007
Tel: 01 53 63 08 74
Metro: Rue du Bac
For other addresses, visit:
www.paulsmith.co.uk

That Haute-Couture High

[1] Alexis Mabille

Situated in the 7th arrondissement's most fashionable shopping street, this store is famous for its bow-tie collection. There are also silk dresses, chic jeans, belts, silk scarves, jewellery and bags.

Having learned his trade at Christian Dior, Yves Saint Laurent and Lancôme, Alexis Mabille started designing unisex clothing and in 2005 launched his own prêt-à-porter and haute couture range.

A fine purveyor of frock coats, white poplin shirts, asymmetrical tunics, crepe sheath dresses and bustiers for today's princesses!

− 11, rue de Grenelle, 75007
Tel: 01 42 22 15 29
Metro: Sèvres-Babylone
For another address, visit:
www.alexismabille.com

Parisian Chic

[2] Carven

Created in 1945, Carmen de Tommaso's label became a leading light of haute couture before launching into prêt-à-porter to produce more spontaneous styles better suited to women's daily lives.

In 2009, Guillaume Henry took over as artistic director, and ever since his style has been casual yet sophisticated, introducing prints and vivid colours. While skirts shortened, his cuts also developed a surprising graphic dimension.

Rehabilitating the French-preppy-look, he went onto create an attractive combination of tradition and avant-garde.

In 2012, he designed his first men's collection and today Carven reaches out to a broad audience in Paris, New York, and Tokyo.

− 8, rue Malher, 75004
Tel: 01 42 77 97 65
Metro: Saint-Paul
For other addresses, visit: www.carven.fr

Chic and Off-Beat

Marc Jacobs

With its white walls, wooden shelves and large bay-windows looking onto the Palais Royal gardens, Marc Jacob's wonderful world finds the perfect peaceful and simple setting for his funky, trashy, chic style – polka dots, course hemlines and oversize buttons – allying gentle American eccentricity with Parisian elegance.

The designer has since elaborated on a whole host of similar concepts: Marc Jacobs; the cooler Marc by Marc Jacobs; Stinky Rat and Little Marc Jacobs for kids, not forgetting Coty's *eau de toilette* based on basil, ivy, orange and daisies.

− 34, rue de Montpensier, 75001
Tel: 01 55 35 02 60
Metro: Palais-Royal
For other addresses, visit:
www.marcjacobs.com

$\frac{2}{1|1}$

Architecture and Hospitality

[1] Maison Rabih Kayrouz

Rabih Kayrouz's workshop-boutique is tucked away in the beautifully paved courtyard that once housed the former Petit Théâtre de Babylone.

His hospitality is excellent, and if available, the Lebanese designer will greet you in person. Having graduated from the *Chambre syndicale de la haute couture parisienne* in 1994, four years later, Rabih Kayrouz created his own studio in Beirut then returned to Paris in 2009 to design prêt-à-porter. His tunic dresses and smocks are a huge hit.

— 38, boulevard Raspail, 75007
Tel: 01 45 48 21 00
Metro: Rue du Bac
www.maisonrabihkayrouz.com

Bohemian Chic

[2] Tsumori Chisato

Tsumori Chisato is the most Parisian Japanese designer in town. After studying at the Bunka Fashion College, Tokyo, Tsumori Chisato worked with Issey Miyake until 1977 before moving to Paris in 2003.

Since then, she has opened over forty retail outlets world-wide, in Asia, the United States, Russia, Italy and Scandinavia.

Designed by Christian Biecher, her boutique in the heart of the fashionable Marais shopping district caters in poetic Bohemian fashions – fine muslin fabrics, deconstructed forms, colourful embroideries, and light-hearted prints bursting with colour and *joie de vivre*.

— 20, rue Barbette, 75003
Tel: 01 42 78 18 88
Metro: Saint-Paul
www.tsumorichisato.com

Paris will always be Paris!

Paris is an exciting melting-pot of experimentation and creativity with a huge appeal to non-French graduate designers who come to the capital in search of fame and glory. The list is endless: the Chinese-American **Alexander Wang**, former artistic director of Balanciaga; the Belgian **Cédric Charlier**, who created a range for La Redoute; the Italian **Marco Zanini**, artistic director of Elsa Schiaparelli's collections; the Italian **Giambattista Valli** of Moncler's Gamme rouge range; **Adeline André**, costume creator for the theatre and opera; the Brazilian **Gustavo Lins**, who created a porcelain dress at the Sèvres manufactory in January 2012; the French-Chinese **Yiqing Yin** and her sculpted clothing; the Lebanese **Elie Saab**, and the Moroccan **Boucha Jarrar** who, in 2010, founded his own fashion house after working for Balanciaga, Scherrer, and Lacroix.

Fifties Passion

¹ Renaissance

Created by Corinne Than Trong in 1989, Renaissance offers jewellery and haute couture by Christian Dior, Elsa Schiaparelli, Yves Saint Laurent, Lanvin, Givenchy, Cardin, etc, as well as luxury vintage accessories including Hermès purses.

Than Trong is an aficionado of 1950s fashion, and her understated, chic boutique nestles elegantly among rue de Beaune's prestigious antique dealers in the heart of the Carré Rive Gauche, the Left Bank's gallery district.

- 14, rue de Beaune, 75007
Tel: 01 42 60 95 49
Metro: Rue du Bac
www.renaissance75007.com

Second-Hand Luxury

² Dépôt Vente Luxe

Light-years from the usual thrift store, Dépôt Vente Luxe is a luxury resale outlet. Its collections of second-hand clothing, outfits, jewellery, purses, belts, fashion accessories and vintage haute couture feature only the best: Chanel, Hermès, Gucci, Yves Saint, Laurent, Prada, Mugler, Céline, Chloé and more besides.

Opened in 1993, the store now has an online store.

- 171, rue de Grenelle, 75007
Tel: 01 45 55 63 47
Metro: La Tour-Maubourg
www.mondepotvente.com

Haute Couture at a Bon Prix

³ La Jolie Garde-Robe

A unique boutique offering an eclectic panorama of everything fashion from the 1900s to the 1980s.

If it is good-as-new vintage skirts, dresses, jackets, blouses, suits, shoes, and children's clothing you are looking for, La Jolie Garde-Robe is ideal, with prices generally around one-hundred and fifty euros (£100/$170).

There are rarities from the 1950s and 1960s to be found and, on a lucky day, you'll discover haute couture dresses at unbeatable prices.

- 15, rue Commines, 75003
Tel: 01 42 72 13 90
Metro: Saint-Sébastien-Froissard

$\frac{1}{1}\left|\frac{2}{2}\right.$

So *romantique*!

¹ L'Ibis rouge

In a small store tucked between the Bon Marché and Saint-Germain-des-Prés, the director, Vivianne Dendievel, a former antiques dealer, reveals her passion for one-offs, originals, jewellery and vintage haute-couture accessories. He also has a penchant for wedding dresses, hats, bags, veils and antique lace.

A boutique that exudes the ephemeral beauty of life's great moments.

— 35, boulevard Raspail, 75007
 Tel: 01 45 48 98 21
 Metro: Sèvres-Babylone

A Museum to Fashion

² Didier Ludot

Looking out onto the Palais-Royal gardens, this gallery-boutique dedicated to luxury vintage fashions showcases decades of haute couture history: coats, dresses, accessories, bags, shoes, leather goods, jewellery and men's clothing.

When he created the gallery in 1975, Didier Ludot was looking for a less formal context for luxury goods, haute couture and vintage clothing.

Since then, his store has developed a reputation as a destination for special events, such as his legendary fashion shows.

— 24, galerie Montpensier, 75001
 Tel: 01 42 96 06 56
 Metro: Palais-Royal
 www.didierludot.fr

Flea Market Special!

Let us introduce two delightful must-visit haunts at the Saint-Ouen flea market in the **Marché Serpette**, both warm and hospitable havens to haute couture. Firstly **Artémise et Cunégonde** (lane 1, stand 28), purveying dresses, coats, blouses, accessories, negligees, vintage purses and jewellery from the 1920s to the present day, with some designer labels. The boutique is a delightful galleria through which to rummage for precious gems. Its treasures are also to be found on the store's internet site. A similar atmosphere can be found at **Patricia Attwood**'s boutique (lane 2, stand 7) – a sixties-style space, offering rare jewels, original bags, Christian Dior blouses, Yves Saint Laurent dresses and jackets, all high-quality and at very reasonable prices.

Chic and Sexy

[1] Chantal Thomass

Beyond her timeless range of sensual lingerie, famous for its refinement, elegance and humour, Chantal Thomass is also an icon of prêt-à-porter; a designer who is unique in her genre and who brings out the provocative best from women with class.

In her boudoir-boutique, pink is the *mot du jour*. There are also delicate, sexy accessories in keeping with the Thomass spirit, like mules and umbrellas. Her bras, suspenders, corsets, waspies, stockings, and lace tights, with flounces and frills are part of the true Parisienne's essential armoury.

- 211, rue Saint-Honoré, 75001
  Tel: 01 42 60 40 56
  Metro: Tuileries
  www.chantalthomass.fr

Tender Pastels

La Paresse en douce

Jeanne Haddad's calm boutique is full of everything she likes, especially bed linen and home accessories, in authentic materials, all in trend-setting monochrome tones.

There are quilt covers, sheets, pillowcases, table mats, towels, slippers and socks, silk pyjamas, cashmere blankets, lingerie, candles and even porcelain tea sets, mainly supplied from Italy. Many of her wares can be made-to-measure.

- 97, rue du Bac, 75007
  Tel: 01 42 22 64 10
  Metro: Rue du Bac

A Short History of the Waspie *à la Française*

The French perfumer and couturier Marcel Rochas designed the first French-style waspie (or *guèpière*, a bustier with garters) for Mae West in the post-WWII period. Christian Dior then created his own version to emphasize shapely shoulders, curvaceous hips and slender waists and incorporated it into his New Look – in his words, 'There can be no fashion without underwear.' The French-style waspie boomed with the technological revolution, and nylon brought stretchier, lighter and sexier garments. Chantal Thomass restored the *guèpière*'s respectability and other couturiers followed suit, like Jean Paul Gaultier who designed them for Madonna's live shows, making the 'wasp-waist' trendier than ever.

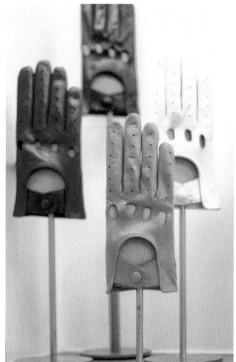

Heads Up!

¹ La Cerise sur le chapeau

Superb felt hats and panamas, for men and women, in a palette of monochrome and rainbow colours. Your head need never feel naked again. The label also has an online store where you'll find the timeless felt 'Trendy' for winter or a delicate straw chapeau for summer.

There are also delightful contemporary versions of classic head-wear. Simply choose your colour, your ribbon and band, and your new millinery masterpiece will be ready in an hour.

– 11, rue Cassette, 75006
Tel: 01 45 49 90 53
Metro: Saint-Sulpice
www.lacerisesurlechapeau.com

Hand in Glove

² Maison Fabre

The Fabre story began in 1924 in the small town of Millau in the Aveyron region, which from the 1930s to 1970s was considered the international capital of glove-making. Étienne Fabre's speciality was white kid gloves. He entrusted the business to his son Denis and his daughter-in-law Rose who developed the establishment's reputation worldwide, working alongside the greats such as Christian Dior.

Since then, Chantal Thomass has created a range for the store while their craftsmanship adorned the hands of Nicole Kidman in Grace Kelly, who was also an avid aficionado of Fabre gloves. Of special note is their re-creation of the magic gloves that feature in *Beauty and the Beast* by Jean Cocteau, who also lived at Palais-Royal. No surprise then that the capital's most handsome pair of mitts are to be found beneath the Palais Royal arcades.

– 128-129, galerie de Valois, 75001
Tel: 01 42 60 75 88
Metro: Palais-Royal
www.maisonfabre.com

Ready to Dance

Repetto

The 6th arrondissement boutique is the smaller version of its elder sibling on rue de la Paix nearby l'Opéra, created in 1947 by Rose Repetto, the mother of the choreographer and dancer Roland Petit. Crammed with tutus and ballet shoes, it is every little girl's dream.

In 2012, they even introduced their own prêt-à-porter collection with graceful supple lines in comfortable fabrics befitting ballerinas.

There are also outdoor shoes, purses, perfumes and customized ballet shoes. The store has also worked alongside many famous couturiers.

– 51, rue du Four, 75006
Tel: 01 45 44 98 65
Metro: Saint-Sulpice
For other addresses, visit: www.repetto.fr

Concept à la Mode

[1] Colette

Colette's is the last word in the latest in-thing – for fashion, literature, perfume, music, beauty, design ...

Created in 1997 by Colette Rousseaux and her daughter Sarah Andelman, the store excels in one-offs and limited series and is a vast emporium of pure joy filled with everyone's favourite brands: Adidas, Burberry, Lacoste, J.M. Weston, Moncler, Nokai, Yazbukey, and Petit Bateau. The window displays and shelves change each week.

⌐ 213, rue Saint-Honoré, 75001
Tel: 01 55 35 33 90
Metro: Tuileries or Pyramides
www.colette.fr

Red Sole Satisfaction

[2] Christian Louboutin

The designer Christian Louboutin opened his first boutique in 1992; he now has over one hundred around the world, including several exclusively dedicated to men's fashion. His eclectic inspirations have led to collaborations with the legendary Crazy Horse cabaret and Walt Disney Studios.

He has also worked on projects with the stars of music, art and cinema, while for Ladurée, Louboutin has created a *macaron* perfume and a box collection. 2014 saw the launch of Christian Louboutin Beauté, a homage to feminine beauty, including Rouge Louboutin, his first nail varnish.

⌐ 38-40, rue de Grenelle, 75007
Tel: 01 42 22 33 07
Metro: Rue du Bac
For other addresses, visit:
www.christianlouboutin.com

Excellence is Everything

[3] Goyard

La Maison Goyard has resided its legendary boutique at 233, rue Saint-Honoré for 180 years, making it the oldest baggage emporium in Paris.

There is luggage, leather goods, and animal accessories as well as a timeless range of products made from the establishment's own emblematic Goyardine canvas created by Edmond Goyard, the manufacturing process of which remains a jealously guarded secret. Perpetuating its tradition of excellence, Goyard offers unique services such as customized trunks and luggage marking. Your wish, however bizarre, is their command.

⌐ 233, rue Saint-Honoré, 75001
Tel: 01 42 60 57 04
Metro: Tuileries
www.goyard.com

$\frac{3}{2\,|\,1}$

$\frac{1}{2|2}$

Sewing Accessories
¹ La Droguerie

The first Parisian store opened in 1975 and was met with such success that the concept spread around the globe. The brand now has huge appeal in Japan since the Japanese first store opened in 1992.

La Droguerie is where amateur seamstresses and jewelers score their fix of beads, buttons, ribbons, braid and threads in an amazing range of materials and colours. Naturally, there are books and knitting patterns and jewellery kits, collections for kids and dolls clothing for the store's latest addition, Perlette.

– 9-11, rue du Jour, 75001
Tel: 01 45 08 93 27
Metro: Les Halles
www.ladroguerie.com

Ruban chic
² Mokuba

In Japanese, *mokuba* means 'rocking horse', but for fans of fashionable frills, it's an essential address for quality ribbonry. Located in the heart of Montorgueil (between Les Halles and place des Victoires), this chic haberdashery is the odd-man-out in a district better known for its fashion outlets and trendy eateries.

The walls abound with ribbons, braids, lace and tassels, all in rolls, aligned like library books, and classified by material, style and colour.

The elegant vendors will unfurl and daintily snip your selection before tucking it into recycled-paper pouches as though each item they touch is a rare and precious treasure. A sheer delight.

– 18, rue Montmartre, 75001
Tel: 01 40 13 81 41
Metro: Étienne-Marcel
www.mokuba.fr

Left Bank
Arty Dandy

In the heart of the fabric district, Arty Dandy is the most with-it concept store in Saint-Germain-des-Prés.

The store's dandy, arty display presents the crème de la crème of the fashion, design and art world: wooden glasses by Waiting for the Sun, wedge sandals by Charles Jourdan, Melys handbags by Kate Lee, Anne Thomas jewellery, Briston watches, as well as artworks, stationery, key-rings, purses, perfumed candles and Ladurée shopping bags.

Each week the boutique's e-store spotlights new-arrivals.

– 1, rue de Furstenberg, 75006
Tel: 01 43 54 00 36
Metro: Saint-Germain-des-Prés
For other addresses, visit:
www.artydandy.com

Floral Finery
[1] Dior Joaillerie
by Victoire de Castellane

If you like your jewellery weird and wonderful, then Dior Joaillerie is not for you. Victoire de Castellane has been the artistic director of Dior's jewellery since 1998 and has a very different vision of her art.

She set out freshen up luxury jewellery and revolutionize its codes and in the process created divine floral broaches, sculpted rings, feathered fountain necklaces, ribbons and bows combining precious stones and cameos such as amethyst, aquamarine, and natural beryl. Look out for the Dear Dior collection, with its haute-couture quality, and the Rose Dior Bagatelle collection, a tribute to Christian Dior's own passion for his rose garden.

⌐ 8, place Vendôme, 75001
Tel: 01 42 96 30 84
Metro: Opéra
www.dior.com

Fearless Finery
[2] La Galerie parisienne

In La Galerie Parisienne, you'll find lamps, glasses and folding screens by designers such as Maria Pergay, Alicia Moï and Aline Gagnaire.

There is also superb jewellery from the early 20th century to the present day, including wonderful rarities such as a Bulgari chain, a René Boivin bracelet, a Van Cleef & Arpels set, a Charles X bracelet, a Georges Fouquet broach from 1900, a Raymond Templier pendant from the 1930s, and many other treasures besides.

The gallery also presents less orthodox creations such as Claude Pelletier's *Tour de Babel* ring and wonderful broaches by Claude Lalanne. Finery with finesse and character!

⌐ 26, rue de Seine, 75006
Tel: 01 43 29 92 18
Metro: Saint-Germain-des-Prés
www.lagalerieparisienne.fr

Oceans of Pearls
[3] Mikimoto

Situated on one of Paris's most elegant squares, Mikimoto purveys the finest selection of cultured pearls in the world. Its felt-lined drawers harbor necklaces, rings, chains, and earrings inlaid with Akoya pearls, baroque pearls, black, white and gold pearls from the southern seas, and more.

Kokichi Mikimoto invented the cultured pearl in 1893 and opened his first boutique in the fashionable Ginza district of Tokyo in 1899. Since then, his outlets have grown, like pearls, around the world.

⌐ 8, place Vendôme, 75001
Tel: 01 42 60 33 55
Metro: Opéra
www.mikimoto.fr

Gorgeous Gems
¹ Marie-Hélène de Taillac

Whether its rings, earrings, fishnet wrist gloves, rainbow necklaces, Marie-Hélène de Taillac's creations are unique. They are often copied but never matched. Her aquamarines, amethysts, citrines, crystals, diamonds and garnets shimmer like celestial candies and are sold in old-school patinated leather jewellery cases engraved with your initials, or a friend's …
What's more, her fascinating website is crammed with information about each stone's specific powers and virtues.

– 8, rue de Tournon, 75006
Tel: 01 44 27 07 07
Metro: Odéon
www.mariehelenedetaillac.com

Natural Finery
² Naïla de Monbrison

Whether gold, copper or stainless steel, Naïla de Monbrison loves metal and works in glass and wood to create expressive jewellery bearing hidden worlds, secrets and emotions. The designer advocates a different vision of matter and fashions for women who seek art rather than decoration.

Hence her ethnic jewellery often accompanies exhibitions by artists such as Taher Chemirik, Catherine Le Gal or Géraldine Luttenbacher.

– 6, rue de Bourgogne, 75007
Tel: 01 47 05 11 15
Metro: Varenne
www.naila-de-monbrison.com

Tiny Treasures
Junko Yamada

Junko Yamada's tiny workshop-boutique is an Aladdin's cave of precious and semi-precious stones, much loved by our Japanese friends.
Formerly a fashion designer, Junko Yamada now creates special edition costume jewellery using traditional and contemporary methods evocative of the enchanting East. Her world is delicate, romantic, poetic and above all, *minuscule*, i.e. *kawaii* – cute and adorable.

– 10, rue de Poitou, 75003
Tel: 01 44 78 08 48
Metro: Filles du Calvaire
or Saint-Sébastien-Froissard

Natural Care
[1] Shu Uemura

With its transparent storefront and minimalist black and white interior designed by Le Corbusier's close friend Jean-Louis Véret, Shu Uemura's salon is elegant and minimalist. The boutique offers natural Japanese beauty care and accessories in the heart of Paris.

Her first boutique, Japan Makeup, created in 1967, became Shu Uemura Cosmetics in 1982, and since then Shu Uemura has developed a series of trademark products such as make-up removing oil, the first foundation stick and a beauty care range based on traditional Chinese medicine.

Among her famous aficionados are Madonna, who commissioned a pair of faux-mink and diamond eyelashes, and Karl Lagerfeld, who having contributed his own range in 2012, added a special collection for his cat, Choupette.

— 176, boulevard Saint-Germain, 75006
Tel: 01 45 48 02 55
Metro: Saint-Germain-des-Prés
For other addresses, visit:
www.shuuemura.com

A Temple to Beauty
Sephora

Paris's leading perfumery and beauty care chain and a glittering showcase to the world's most prestigious perfumes – Guerlain, Givenchy, Christian Dior …

Wander at will around the vast Champs-Élysées boutique and try their tantalizing products. There are also beauty and styling bars dispensing hair or nail care for in-store, on-the-spot pampering. Look out for Ladurée's own Les Merveilleuses cosmetics range.

— 70-72, avenue des Champs-Élysées, 75008
Tel: 01 53 93 22 50
Metro: George-V or Franklin D. Roosevelt
For other addresses, visit: www.sephora.fr

Plant power
Aesop

Created in Melbourne in 1987, a range of Australian beauty products for indulging your hair, your body and your mind. Their skin-care range is sublime, especially the mandarine moisturizer. The products are natural, delicately perfumed and brimming with antioxidants, while the minimalist interior décor is also made from natural materials.

Look out for the magnificent Marrakech Intense eau de toilette.

— 20, rue Bonaparte, 75006
Tel: 01 44 41 02 19
Metro: Saint-Germain-des-Prés
For other addresses, visit: www.aesop.com

$\frac{1}{1}\Big|\frac{1}{1}$

Aromas from the Past and Beyond

[1] Buly

Inaugurated in 1787, the Bully official dispensary became famous in the 19th century for Jean-Vincent Bully's famous 'vinaigre de toilette'. Today Buly (single 'l') is a temple to the bouquets of yesteryear and to the innovations of today.

The alchemists-in-chief, Mssrs Victoire de Taillac and Ramdane Touhami, create delicate symphonies of essential authentic fragrances, ministering oils, clays, scents and powders stored in huge jars. There are also candles, elegantly packaged soaps, Eastern incenses and perfumed safety matches.

With its marble counters, Tuscany stone floor, 18th century furniture and antique portraits, the boutique presents a poetic paean to the past.

– 6, rue Bonaparte, 75006
Tel: 01 43 29 02 50
Metro: Saint-Germain-des-Prés
www.buly1803.com

Memories of Times Gone By

Frédéric Malle

In 2000, Frédéric Malle introduced a completely novel approach to perfume. In resistance to the intensely marketed brands, he asked the world's greatest noses to produce their own signature scents under their own names.

The result is a range of 'minimal perfumes' that love their wearer's skin. 'Angéliques sous la Pluie' by Jean-Claude Ellena, 'Dans tes Bras' by Maurice Roucel, 'Lipstick Rose' by Ralf Schwieger – evocative names for evocative fragrances. There are scented candles – our favourites: 'Saint des Saints' by Carlos Benaïm and 'Un Gardénia la Nuit' by Dominique Ropion.

– 21, rue du Mont-Thabor, 75001
Tel: 01 42 22 16 89
Metro: Tuileries or Concorde
For other addresses, visit:
www.fredericmalle.com

Florence in Paris

[2] Amin Kader

Alongside his leather goods, clothing and accessories, the couturier Amin Kader is an official distributor of beauty products from the *Officina Profumo Farmaceutica di Santa Maria Novella di Firenze* founded in 1612, a descendant of Florence's Dominican pharmaceutical tradition.

In a kitsch chapel setting, you'll find perfumes, creams, pots-pourris, balms and soaps in delectable paper packaging lined with dried roses. For a real trip back in time, try the Renaissance rice powder deployed by ladies of the period as well as the famous Acqua di Colonia. Pamper yourself with soft silk scarves and gentle caressing cashmeres. Or if you're looking for rarities, try the perfumed handkerchiefs and iris-flower toothpaste.

– 2, rue Guisarde, 75006
Tel: 01 43 26 27 37
Metro: Saint-Germain-des-Prés
For other address, visit: www.aminkader.fr

Décoration

{ Interior Design }

Looking for classic tables or designer chairs? Exotic art objects?
Candles and fragrances? Elegant tableware? Porcelain decorations
or crystal lamp fittings? Auctioneers or florists? Ladurée has all
the names you'll need for creating enchanting interiors. Ladurée
adores décor and here we reveal our suppliers – the sources of the
fabrics, paints, wallpapers, stuccos and chandeliers that decorate
our tearooms. We also share the antique dealers and flea markets
where we hunt down our antique furniture, designer ornaments
and contemporary art.

Baccarat, Bernardaud, Christofle: three of the world's finest purveyors of crystal, porcelain and silver ware – perfect for setting festive tables or offering gifts to treasure. If it's auctioneers you prefer, Hotel Drouot and Artcurial regularly organize sales of furniture, paintings, books, tableware, archaeology, prints or antique fabrics, from prestigious or anonymous collections.

... MAISON BACCARAT ...

Once home to Marie-Laure de Noailles, one of the 20th century's most daring and influential patrons of the arts, the Maison Baccarat was redesigned by Philippe Starck. Everything here is astounding: from the majestic staircase crowned by a huge, gently revolving crystal chandelier to the crystal tableware, light fittings and jewellery. The store is composed of succession of salons, with a vast ballroom and the Baccarat museum on the second floor. In its setting of red bricks, wainscoting and gilt features, the Cristal Room restaurant serves a divine menu created by the Michelin-starred chefs Guy Martin and Adrien Manac'h. An extraordinary temple of beauty!

– 11, place des États-Unis, 75116 🕊 Tel: 01 40 22 11 00 🕊 Metro: Boissière
🕊 For other addresses, visit: www.baccarat.fr

... BERNARDAUD ...

A family affair founded in 1863, Bernardaud supplies contemporary creations and historical reproductions of tableware and decorative objects. Here you'll find 'Les Tasses Historiques' and 'Botanique' collections, exquisitely crafted tea and dinner services from the 18th century, identically reproduced by their original creators, the French monarchy's own manufactory, the *Manufacture Royale*. In both Parisian boutiques, as well as the large department stores, you'll also find limited editions, porcelain jewellery and their magnificent lithophanes illuminated by delicately perfumed candles.

– 11, rue Royale, 75008 and 60, rue Mazarine, 75006 🕊 Tel: 01 47 42 82 66 and 01 46 33 94 36
🕊 Metro: Concorde and Saint-Germain-des-Prés
🕊 For other addresses, visit: www.bernardaud.fr

⋯ CHRISTOFLE ⋯

Since its creation in 1830, Christofle has remained loyal to its deep love of the beauty of silver and its rue Royale boutique, opened in 1897, is a unique showcase to its wonders: birth gifts, pens, candelabras, photo frames and rings, especially the 925 range, designed by Andrée Putman in 2005. Over the years, Christofle has produced silverware for the rich and powerful, for example the four-thousand solid-silver piece honorary dinner service commissioned by Napoleon III for the Tuileries Palace, a work redolent of today's exquisite designs.

⁻ 9, rue Royale, 75008 ⤙ Tel: 01 55 27 99 13 ⤙ Metro: Concorde
⤙ For other addresses, visit: www.christofle.com

⋯ HÔTEL DROUOT ⋯

Hôtel Drouot is a godsend for Ladurée and has oft provided the furnishings necessary to decorate our tearooms. Sitting proudly in a district crammed with art galleries and antiques emporiums, Paris's leading auctioneer is an Ali Baba's cave for bargain hunters. The excitement builds early in the day and soon after opening you'll already find its succession of exhibition rooms, from the basement to the upper-floors, crowded with silent buyers eagerly seeking out rare gems from any period from the 17th century to the present day: furniture, painting, silverware, decorative objects, light fittings, engravings, scores, carpets, or haute-couture. There is always the possibility that you'll find the dresser of your dreams at an affordable price; the thrill of the hunt is exquisite.

⁻ 9, rue Drouot, 75009 ⤙ Tel: 01 48 00 20 20 ⤙ Metro: Richelieu-Drouot ⤙ www.drouot.com

⋯ ARTCURIAL ⋯

Located in the Hotel Marcel Dassault at the corner of the avenue Montaigne and the avenue des Champs-Élysées, Artcurial is another of Paris's leading auction houses. In its succession of muted galleries you will find regular exhibitions of furniture, *objets d'art*, curiosities, watches, photographs, wine, and original cartoons. There are also experts on hand to tell you whether your grandmother's clock is indeed a valuable treasure or not. On the first floor, there is even a marvellous bookstore specializing in art, architecture, fashion and design, including an annotated catalogue and out-of-print section. And the icing on the cake? A delightful, distinctly Parisian cafe.

⁻ 7-9, rond-point des Champs-Élysées, 75008 ⤙ Tel: 01 42 99 20 20
⤙ Metro: Franklin D. Roosevelt ⤙ www.artcurial.com

Homage to Nature
[1] Deyrolle

From the sidewalk, this curiosity shop, opened in 1831, looks like a nirvana for natural history lovers.

On the creaking floorboards upstairs prowl tigers, lions and white bears for hire or purchase, while the charming antique counters display nature's rarities: shells, minerals, fossils and insects.

Downstairs, you'll find garments by the Prince Jardinier boutique, a brand of clothing made from natural fibres and chic gardening accessories, designed by Louis Albert de Broglie. There are also books and gardening aids.

A boutique-museum that is at once extraordinary, enchanting and enlightening.

— 46, rue du Bac, 75007
Tel: 01 42 22 30 07
Metro: Rue du Bac
www.deyrolle.com

Gustavian Style
[2] Astier de Villatte

A boutique with retro charm on the doorstep of the Palais-Royal, facing a coffee-roasting establishment producing one of the finest javas in town. Here you'll find fine ceramic tableware, cutlery, incense, scented candles, pampille chandeliers, mouldings, stationery, beauty creams, *eaux de Cologne* in beautiful vintage bottles and even designer dish soap.

The patinated and blanched Gustavian furniture brings an 18th-century elegance to the interior, enhancing the overall charm of a delightful haunt.

— 173, rue Saint-Honoré, 75001
Tel: 01 42 60 74 13
Metro: Tuileries or Palais-Royal
www.astierdevillatte.com

Nordic Vintage
[3] Les Fées

With her second emporium, 'Avec Les Fées', Sylvie Aubry, the florist at Paris's exclusive hôtel Meurice, again brings her own distinctive touch to bear: a collection of vintage Nordic furnishings, antique and contemporary porcelain, floral compositions, glassware, cloches in all forms (look out for the roast chicken model), and a treasure trove of delightful gifts to offer your hostess at last-minute dinner invitations.

There is a bewitching poetry about the boutique, enhanced by the beautiful vaulted cellar containing the Toiles du Soleil collection of plant-motif shopping bags, lamps and other curiosities.

— 19, rue Charlot, 75003
Tel: 01 43 70 14 76
Metro: Saint-Sébastien-Froissard

$\frac{1}{2}\Big|\frac{1}{2}$

Between Art and Design
¹ Sentou

An intimate two-storey boutique where for over twenty years Pierre Romanet has been dispensing legendary creations by avant-garde designers and artists: light fittings by Isamu Noguchi, ceramics by Brigitte de Bazelaire, fine porcelain by Tse & Tse, glasses by Claudio Colucci, the M400 sculptural staircase by Roger Tallon and much more besides.

The *crème de la crème* of furniture, lighting, tableware and textiles. Look out for his other Parisian addresses.

— 26, boulevard Raspail, 75007
Tel: 01 45 49 00 05
Metro: Rue du Bac
For other addresses, visit: www.sentou.fr

Wandering East
² Liwan

Liwan is a collaboration of three designers, Lina Audi, Christine Bergstrom and Dina Haidar. Their small boutique near Saint-Sulpice Church offers everything from tableware and kitchen utensils to clothing and accessories with an Eastern touch.

The trio devise their own household items – table linen, cushions, luxury velvet and silk fabrics, sandals and earrings – and their designs are produced by traditional craftsmen in Lebanon.

Alongside their own productions, the boutique also offers glassware, embroidered sheets, kaftans and alabasters from North Africa, India, Greece and Egypt.

— 8, rue Saint-Sulpice, 75006
Tel: 01 43 26 07 40
Metro: Mabillon or Odéon

The World at Home
The Conran Shop

Founded in England in 1973 by Terence Conran, the Conran Shop has become a veritable institution. A leader in the world of design and creation, it offers vintage and contemporary furniture, tableware, kitchen utensils, books, gifts, bags, luggage, cosmetics, watches, jewellery, toys and books.

Just opposite the Bon Marché, Paris's chicest department store, the Conran Shop should be the first port of call for design shopping, especially for novices.

— 117, rue du Bac, 75007
Tel: 01 42 84 10 01
Metro: Rue du Bac
or Metro: Sèvres-Babylone
www.conranshop.fr

Folk Art
¹ La Tuile à loup

La Tuile à Loup is the Parisian showcase of France's poetic provincial charm – purveying traditional regional craftsmanship, especially from the Alsace and Provence regions.

You'll find beautifully crafted, often unique, household items that are a pleasure to hold and behold. There are dishes and plates, terrines and soup dishes, finials and garden vases in varnished terracotta or sandstone, often with animal themes.

You'll also find wickerwork baskets and trays and table linen with motifs, as well as regular temporary art exhibitions.

— 35, rue Daubenton, 75005
Tel: 01 47 07 28 90
Metro: Censier-Daubenton
www.latuilealoup.com

Wedding Lists
² Au Bain Marie

Created in 1977 by Aude Clément, Au Bain Marie has everything you need to entertain in style; it is also perfect for wedding, birthday or Saint Valentine's Day gifts.

A gorgeous blend of 17th century, Art Deco, Orientalist, and Japanese decorative genres, the store is a treasure trove of tableware, especially its regal silverware collections including everything from cutlery to work tables, dessert cloches, and champagne buckets.

You'll also find crystal, pewter, earthenware, and fine porcelain, as well as cookery books, tea-caddies and even hunting, mountain-trekking and sea-faring equipment. For the thriftier buyer there is also a vast selection of decorative delights for under sixty euros (£50/$65).

— 56, rue de l'Université, 75007
Tel: 01 42 71 08 69
Metro: Rue du Bac
www.aubainmarie.com

Antiques and Curios
³ Galerie Salon

The Street, painted by the figurative artist Balthus, shows that the current gallery was once a hairdresser's salon.

Hence the name of the gallery. Its owners, Carole and Stéphane Borraz, formerly operated from the Saint-Ouen flea market and today present Scandinavian antiques, French and Italian provincial furniture, folk art, paintings, antique toys and other curios. There are also contemporary creations – perfume, jewellery, such as Astier de Villatte's sublime eaux de Cologne, Emma Cassi jewellery, Kühn Keramik ceramics, Tse & Tse furnishings, Apolline à Paris textiles, Sophie Digard scarves, and Happy To See You fabric dolls, that little girls adore.

— 4, rue Bourbon-le-Château, 75006
Tel: 06 33 85 98 99
Metro: Mabillon
www.galeriesalon.fr

$$\frac{1}{2\,|\,3}$$

From Season to Season

[1] Au fil des couleurs

Au Fil des Couleurs offers a large choice of rare wallpapers as well as upholstery and décor accessories by Cole & Son, Osborne & Little, Sandberg, Miss Print and Adrienne Neff.

The wallpaper range is eclectic: tile-imitation, exotic motifs, fifties prints, and a Richard Saja *toile de Jouy*. The store has thousands of references to peruse *in situ* as well as an exhaustive online magazine presenting all the current collections.

A rare French wallpaper specialist that regularly renews its collections according to the seasons and current in-vogue colours.

— 31, rue de l'Abbé-Grégoire, 75006
Tel: 01 45 44 74 00
Metro: Saint-Placide
For other addresses, visit:
www.aufildescouleurs.com

Made in England

[2] Farrow & Ball

Hand-crafted artisanal paints and wallpapers, in intense timeless colours with chalky matte finishes: this is the Farrow and Ball look. Their unique paints are traditionally produced using natural pigments, umbers, chalk, lime, linseed oil, and kaolin produced at their Wimborne manufactory in Dorset, England, as they have been since 1946.

The subtle nuances of grey, beige, yellow, blue and red would transform even the most humble abodes into the *nec plus ultra* of fashion.

Aptly located near the Musée d'Orsay, the boutique offers everything you need to bring colour to every corner of the home.

— 50, rue de l'Université, 75007
Tel: 01 45 44 82 20
Metro: Rue du Bac
For another address, visit:
www.farrow-ball.com

The Colour of Travel

Ressource

The creator Patrick Baty has a passion for the different textures of paint through history from Antiquity to the 19th century. The result is matte, satin or gloss tones with cloud, mineral or patina effects: 'Les Couleurs Historiques' and 'Les Blancs Cassés' ranges are to die for. We also have a soft spot for the Sérénité and Paris Rive Droite–Rive Gauche ranges by the creator and designer Philippe Model, the Cohérence and Confluence collections by interior architect Robert Gervais and a vibrant collection by Serge Bensimon, the founder of the famous Autour du Monde and Home Autour du Monde boutiques.

— 2-4, avenue du Maine, 75015
Tel: 01 42 22 58 80
Metro: Falguière
For another address, visit:
www.ressource-peintures.com

The essentials

Paris's major fabric and textile producers are to be found between rue du Mail and place de Furstenberg, one of Paris's most delightful squares near Saint-Germain-des-Prés. These emporiums of eye-candy purvey magnificent upholstery as well as wallpaper, furnishings and décor accessories that bring homes to life.

··· RUBELLI ···

Velvet, silk, brocade and damask: Rubelli sells hand-made fabrics and historical reproductions using traditional techniques as well as highly sophisticated textiles deploying metallic fibres, embroideries, patina silk, and Jacquards. You'll also find wallpaper by The Walls of Venice and Dominique Kieffer's natural collections. Opposite, Rubelli's sister outlet offers Donghia furnishings and light fittings created in Murano. Founded in Venice in 1858, Rubelli helped restore the Fenice Theatre after its fire and is a partner of the Peggy Guggenheim Collection in Venice. A textile kingdom where quality is king.

⁻ 11, rue de l'Abbaye, 75006   Tel: 01 43 54 27 77   Metro: Saint-Germain-des-Prés
www.rubelli.com

··· PIERRE FREY ···

Founded in 1935, Pierre Frey produces some of the finest fabrics in the world and is an icon of French excellence. His family enterprise designs, creates and distributes fabrics, wallpaper, carpets and even furniture. There are reproductions of 19th century textiles, as well as the latest contemporary styles. Whether ethnic, embroidered, woven, or Indian, here you'll find your heart's desire. Also available are wonderful weaves by Braquenié, Fadini Borghi, Boussac and Le Manach.

⁻ 27, rue du Mail, 75002   Tel: 01 44 77 35 22   Metro: Bourse,   www.pierrefrey.com

··· BRAQUENIÉ ···

Founded in 1824 and bought out by Pierre Frey in 1991, alongside its top-end cottons, Indian fabrics and *toile de Jouy*, Braquenié embodies the essence of French classicism, purveying the 18th and 19th-century fabrics that once decorated the royal residences of the world. Here you'll find reproductions of handwoven textiles, rugs, and carpets which once adorned Emperor Napoleon III's apartments at the Louvre, the Pope's Vatican residence, Victor Hugo's home in Paris and the Petit Trianon at Versailles – the list is endless. Take a trip into the sumptuous past and treat yourself to the luxuriance of history at home.

− 3, rue de Furstenberg, 75006 ✎ Tel: 01 44 07 15 37 ✎ Metro: Saint-Germain-des-Prés

✎ www.pierrefrey.com

⋯ LELIÈVRE ⋯

Having recently celebrated its hundredth anniversary in 2014, Lelièvre has an immense reputation around the world. Their magnificent second-floor showroom imparts an incredible range of textiles to suit any style of home: Jacquards, silk velvet, net fabrics, classic solid and semi-plain colours as well as more adventurous designs that shimmer in the light. You'll also find Lyonnaise silk by Tassinari & Chatel, Sonia Rykiel's distinctly girly collections and Jean Paul Gaultier's more cutting edge array among others, as well as cushions, blankets, towels, and more besides. Another of France's excellent traditional family businesses.

− 13, rue du Mail, 75002 ✎ Tel: 01 43 16 88 00 ✎ Metro: Bourse ✎ www.lelievre.eu

⋯ MANUEL CANOVAS ⋯

Stripes, solid-colours and ethnic, exotic and floral motifs in bold, unusual colour combinations; silks, damasks, and toiles de Jouy in warm, vibrant shades of rose Indian, amethyst, anis and turquoise sometimes incorporating prints and embroidery: such is the world of Manuel Canovas, a brand belonging to the English Colefax group who purvey fine fabric collections in infinite tones, reinterpreting the 18th-century spirit of *art-de-vivre*.

− 6, rue de l'Abbaye, 75006 ✎ Tel: 01 43 29 91 36 ✎ Metro: Saint-Germain-des-Prés

✎ www.manuelcanovas.com

⋯ NOBILIS ⋯

Founded by Adolphe Halard in 1928, this elegant showroom in Saint Germain des Prés supplies all your needs in terms of colours, textures, prints and motifs in the home. The fabric range is magnificent: Chinese prints, floral and fifties motifs, moires, and leopard print velvet. You'll also find wallpaper, lace trimmings, and timeless décor accessories, expressionist rugs, elegant furnishings, cushions, blankets, bed covers, perfumed candles and household fragrances.

− 38, rue Bonaparte, 75006 ✎ Tel: 01 43 29 12 71 ✎ Metro: Saint-Germain-des-Prés

✎ For other addresses, visit: www.nobilis.fr

$$\frac{1}{1}\bigg|\frac{1}{1}$$

Contemporary weaves
Dedar

A supremely chic showroom presenting fabrics, wallpapers, and lace trimmings, alongside armchairs, folding screens, and cushions. Their range is vast : over three hundred models in three thousand colours. Dedar extols the virtues of contemporary Italian textiles: sensual shimmering silk and precious fabrics with exuberant graphics.

In 1976 Nicola and Elda Fabrizio opened their first store near Como, Italy. Now run by their children, Caterina and Raffaele, the company has contributed to the decoration of a whole host of famous sites including Paris's Hotel Costes, Dubai's Sky Gardens building, and Joël Robuchon's Atelier restaurant in Las Vegas.

— 20, rue Bonaparte, 75006
Tel: 01 43 25 93 01
Metro: Saint-Germain-des-Prés
www.dedar.com

Italian Fibre
[1] Colony chez Cleo C

Colony specializes in traditionally woven upholstery fabrics such as lampas, velvet, brocade and silk with floral motifs and solid-colours. Their textiles are created on the basis of historical archives from France, Venice, Piedmont and countries further east, and along with reworked designs to suit contemporary styles.

Colony also creates furniture upholstered in their own textiles. Cleo C is Colony's showroom in Paris. The attractive Italian Cleo Carnelli has been living in Paris for years and has a passion for Italian textiles that she loves to share. Expect a warm welcome!

— 30, rue Jacob, 75006
Tel: 01 43 29 61 70
Metro: Saint-Germain-des-Prés
www.colonyfabrics.com

Ecological Craftsmanship
Caravane

Caravane create a beautiful world full of colour, texture and tales of travel. They have their own comprehensive range of household furnishing and accessories: everything from exquisitely comfortable sofas and armchairs, to sheets, bedspreads, sharkskin house linen, curtains, cushions, perfumed candles, and stoneware crockery.

They combine this subtle contemporary approach with ethic prints and motifs discovered on their travels through North Africa, India and Japan: Berber rugs, eiderdowns, Japanese wall lamps and ceiling lights. Simple wares crafted by local artisans in authentic, eco-friendly materials. Their prints are original, their colours warm; everything is finely crafted by local artisans using eco-friendly materials.

— 9, rue Jacob, 75006
Tel: 01 53 10 08 86
Metro: Saint-Germain-des-Prés
For other address, visit:
www.caravane.fr

Haute Couture Carpets
¹ Codimat

In 1955 Codimat took over the Catry carpet factory created in the mid-19th century and ever since Codimat has become a benchmark in top-of-the-range rugs and carpets.

Their range covers staircase carpets, contemporary creations and antique reproductions woven in natural fibres, including aloe vera, nettle and hemp, while some – Mirror of the Orient, Memories of Ispahan and Mystery of the Nile – call to mind more exotic evocations.

The brand also reproduces designs by of the late great 20th-century interior designer Madeleine Castaing, and her famous ocelot rugs – a favourite of Ladurée's.

⁻ 63-65, rue du Cherche-Midi, 75006
Tel: 01 45 44 68 20
Metro: Vaneau or Rennes
www.codimatcollection.com

Stylized Prints
Edmont Petit

Apart from its splendid fabric collections, Edmont Petit distributes textile creations by Madeleine Castaing, the iconic 20th-century interior designer, known for her Castaing blue and her unique decorative style. Castaing bucked the trend by fusing graphic genres, sometimes drawing on less noble yet poetic elements to tell stories.

She designed an exclusive range of motifs for Edmont Petit which are still produced today, among them the Lola Montez or Mac Mahon exuberant leaf motif collections, naturally available in Castaing blue.

⁻ 23, rue du Mail, 75002
Tel: 01 45 14 18 20
Metro: Bourse
www.edmond-petit.fr

The Madeleine-Castaing Style

Known as the 'diva of decoration', the antique dealer and interior designer Madeleine Castaing frequented Montparnasse in its heyday and was a close friend of Amedeo Modigliani and Chaim Soutine. Her work was inspired by neo-classical aesthetics, but unlike others she never succumbed to 18th-century or 2nd-Empire temptations, and avoided the influence of Russian, Swedish and British design. Instead she created her own genuine decorative style, rescuing bamboo, ocelot carpets and fringed armchairs from design obscurity; she is especially known for her colour: Castaing blue. Her unique style has greatly influenced today's great interior designers such as her former student, Jacques Grange.

Like Landscapes
¹ Zuber

One of the world's most famous and time-honoured manufactories, which has been producing paints and wallpapers in its customary fashion at the Rixheim manufactory since 1790. The enchanting Saint Germain des Prés showroom exhibits the full range of Zuber's beautiful wallpapers, silks, upholstery and sumptuous panoramic scenes printed from original plates.

Its archives encompass nearly two hundred and thirty years of production covering everything from ceiling rosaces to leather upholstery, *trompe-l'œils*, drapery and floral borders.

– 12, rue des Saints-Pères, 75007
Tel: 01 42 77 95 91
Metro: Saint-Germain-des-Prés
www.zuber.fr

Historical Wallpaper
² De Gournay

At De Gournay you'll find a world of hand-painted wallpapers, mural scenes and silk fabrics inspired by historical decorative motifs. Look out for the Palais Imperial collection, designed from Japanese prints on folding screens dating from 1590.

The showroom's elegant lay-out presents De Gournay's sofas, armchairs, beds, tables, stools, mirrors, dressers and delicate porcelain to their best advantage. You'll also find a small fashion section.

By the way: De Gournay has designed motifs for the Duchess of Cambridge's dresses created by her favourite designer Jenny Packham. The pinnacle of chic!

– 15, rue des Saints-Pères, 75006
Tel: 01 40 20 08 97
Metro: Saint-Germain-des-Prés
www.degournay.com

Poetry in Plants
The Mauny
Wallpaper Manufactory

Created by André Mauny in 1933, the Mauny wallpaper manufactory near Angers creates handmade wallpapers and fabrics using traditional production processes in their purest form: traditional wood block presses, hand-brushed backgrounds, and stenciled motifs.

Their patterns are a delicate combination of classical bucolic themes, plant and animal motifs with quilt effects. Simple, finely crafted pleasures that bring poetry to even the most humble abode.

– 3, rue des Saints-Pères, 75006
Tel: 01 42 60 67 01
Metro: Saint-Germain-des-Prés
www.manufacture-mauny.fr

A Treasury of Trimmings

¹ Declercq Passementiers

In upholstery and furnishing, trimmings provide that final delicate finish to enhance fine craftsmanship. Founded in 1852, Declercq supplies handmade fringes, tassels, braids and gimps in a range of styles from the classic to the ethnic in a variety of themes and has contributed to major renovation projects of historical buildings and museums.

– 4, rue du Mail, 75002
  Tel: 01 40 39 11 20
  Metro: Sentier
  www.declercqpassementiers.fr

Upholstery Supplies

² Houlès

Created in 1928, Houlès is a family business in Paris's decoration and craft district and has an international reputation for its trimmings.

It also purveys hardware such as curtain rails and stair rods, fabrics for upholstery and curtains, and supplies such as upholstery tools and accessories for the DIY home décor experience.

– 18, rue Saint-Nicolas, 75012
  Tel: 01 43 44 65 19
  Metro: Ledru-Rollin
  For another address, visit: www.houles.com

Bespoke Frames

Baxter

Founded thirty-five years ago, this small atelier-boutique, specializing in antique prints and engravings, is a timeless wonder. Run by Aurélie Flor-Jeanmaire and her husband Jaime Flor, the store sells engravings, decorative plates, architectural scenes and contemporary drawings. All work is original – because Baxter has banished the word 'reproduction' from their vocabulary!

– 15, rue du Dragon, 75006
  Tel: 01 45 49 01 34
  Metro: Saint-Germain-des-Prés

Poetry is in the Detail

Brass

For the past thirty-five years, Brass have been supplying those minor details of décor to be found throughout the house: curtain rails, bathroom fittings, doorknobs, decorative grates, as well as those invisible ironwork accessories like hinges, locks and supports without which the house would fall apart.

Styles vary from the classical, to Art Deco and contemporary; their finishing is sublime. If you design your own doorknob the establishment will make it for you.

– 37, rue des Mathurins, 75008
  Tel: 01 44 67 90 61 (by appointment)
  Metro: Saint-Augustin
  www.brass-quincaillerie.com

An Elegy to the Past

¹ Atelier Prométhée

Terracotta waterspouts and fountains, urns and busts; carved stone statues and marble basins; enamel flooring and tiles, hearths and bas-reliefs: Atelier Prométhée purveys all those classical decorative features usually found in palaces and museums. All their wares are lovingly handmade in their workshops using traditional techniques such as wax or lime-wash patinas; your designs can also be tailor-made.

The owners Cedric Riou and Benoit Ruffenach have worked for national museums and historical monuments, such as the chateau of Versailles, and their workshop has been recognized by the French state for its excellence in heritage conservation.

– 25, rue du Landy,
  93210 La Plaine Saint-Denis
  Tel: 01 49 98 00 36
  RER B La Plaine-Stade de France
  www.atelierpromethee.com

Classical Stuccos

² Auberlet & Laurent

At Auberlet & Laurent you'll find beautiful textured wall and ceiling stuccos: mouldings and rosaces, Art Deco coving, architectural ornamentations, columns, pilasters, steles, plinths and more.

There are exquisite reproductions of Louis XVI, Empire and early 20th century pieces to turn your home into a chateau.

The workshop's output is so historically accurate that it is regularly called up for renovation and heritage projects.

– 8, boulevard du Général-Giraud,
  94100 Saint-Maur-des-Fossés
  Tel: 01 48 85 95 99
  RER A Saint-Maur
  www.auberletetlaurent.com

Plaster Reproductions

Michel Lorenzi

Founded in 1871, this tantalizing temple to the past purveys decorative bas-reliefs and sculptures, antique basins and masks, acanthus leaves and fleurs de lys for hire or purchase.

Its work is so divine that is frequented by filmmakers, photographers and events designers in search of their ideal historical reconstruction. Simply provide a design or photo and Michel Lorenzi will turn it out in plaster, resin or stone. The workshop's artistry is also much sought after by major institutions such as the French National Assembly, the chateau de Compiegne and Caron perfumes.

– 60, avenue Laplace,
  94110 Arcueil
  Tel: 01 47 35 37 54
  RER B Laplace or Arcueil-Cachan
  www.lorenzi.fr

Crystal Magic
[1] Baguès

Founded in 1860, Baguès is a veritable cathedral of light, an emporium where time itself seems to have been suspended.

In their spectacular showroom tucked inside an archway of the 12th arrondissement's delightful Viaduc des Arts, you'll find exquisite bronze and crystal light fittings and chandeliers cascading from the ceiling.

In this theatrical setting, antique reproductions and the finest of today's designer creations sit side-by-side. Iron and bronze are handcrafted in the traditional manner. Every detail is hand-wrought from the crystal settings to the gold-leaf gilding. The establishment also restores ailing chandeliers, light fittings and lamps to their former glory.

⌐ 73, avenue Daumesnil, 75012
Tel: 01 43 41 53 53
Metro: Reuilly-Diderot
www.bagues-france.com

Let There Be Light
Épi Luminaire

A fine purveyor of light in all its forms: chandeliers, fittings, table lamps and floor lamps in crystal and hand-patinated bronze.

You'll also find contemporary designs in glass, metal, wood and synthetic materials, bathroom and exterior lighting and a furniture range. Some of their wares are to be found illuminating Ladurée's tearooms and Paul bakeries.

⌐ 30, cours de Vincennes, 75012
Tel: 01 43 46 11 36
Metro: Nation
www.epiluminaires.fr

That Contemporary Glow
VDE Luminaires

VDE Luminaires are specialists in bespoke lighting, and classic or contemporary creations in glass, brass, bronze, steel and wood. The boutique is a favourite haunt of interior designers working on some of France's most prestigious restaurant and hotel commissions, and you'll find their creations in the Bristol Hotel and Hotel de l'Abbaye in Paris and the Hotel du Palais in Biarritz.

Don't let this discourage you: you'll also find a whole host of beautiful and affordable lamps and fittings to turn even the most humble abode into a palace.

⌐ 26, rue Malar, 75007
Tel: 01 48 05 72 73
Metro: La Tour-Maubourg
www.vdelight.fr

$\frac{1}{1|1}$

The Charm of Yesteryear

[1] Mis en Demeure

Mis en Demeure is a journey into the interior world of grand family homes, replete with children's tea parties and formal dinners.

You'll find provincial-style patinated furniture, Club armchairs, stylish dressers, gilt wood chandeliers, lamps, porcelain, carpets and antique engravings.

Philippe Darrot's second boutique opposite also sells antiques with the same poetic aura.

— 27, rue du Cherche-Midi, 75006
Tel: 01 45 48 83 79
Metro: Sèvres-Babylone
www.misendemeure.com

That Versailles Touch

Jardins du Roi Soleil

Jardins du Roi Soleil sells garden furniture inspired by the decorative arts of the Chateau of Versailles: benches, cast-iron vases, trellis lanterns, and a range of rare plants from the Domaine des Rochettes nursery. Their *piece de resistance* is a patented adaptation of the orange tree boxes used under Louis XIV's reign, originally designed by André Le Notre in 1670.

— 32, boulevard de la Bastille, 75012
Tel: 01 43 44 44 31
Metro: Bastille
www.jardinsduroisoleil.com

French Tradition

Gilles Nouailhac

A specialist in made-to-order armchairs, chairs and sofas of the great French tradition; all pieces are hand-sculpted and traditionally upholstered in the finest fabrics from France's best producers.

The store sells chateau and 18th century reproductions as well as contemporary creations of similar noble distinction.

— 94, rue du Bac, 75007
Tel: 01 53 63 00 25
Metro: Rue du Bac
www.gillesnouailhac.com

Colours of Yesteryear

Moissonnier

Moissonnier is a contemporary design free-zone. Its furniture is purely old-school, exquisitely crafted according the traditions of the past: emerald green dressers, fuchsia armchairs, sky blue sideboards: a rainbow of 18th and 19th century styles.

The establishment also resurrects furniture from forgotten forms of yore, customizing dressers, wing chairs, tables and buffets with the patina and colour of your desires.

— 52, rue de l'Université, 75007
Tel: 01 42 61 84 88
Metro: Rue du Bac
www.moissonnier.com

A Passion for Decorative Arts
¹ Yves Gastou

Since its inception, Yves Gastou's gallery beside the Beaux Arts has been a flagship of 20ᵗʰ century decorative arts. He still presents his early passions: Art nouveau, André Arbus, Gio Ponti, Carlo Scarpa, Ettore Sottsass and the pioneering Alessandro Mendini, but has gradually brought in a contemporary selection of unique pieces by Philippe Hiquily, Maxime Old, Ado Chale, Paul Evans, Emmanuel Babled and Claude de Muzac.

With the same ever-lasting fascination, Yves Gastou and his son Victor present an exceptional panorama of 20ᵗʰ century creations which elevate design to the status of art.

⁻ 12, rue Bonaparte, 75006
Tel: 01 53 73 00 10
Metro: Saint-Germain-des-Prés
www.galerieyvesgastou.com

From Fashion to Design
² Galerie Clémande

Nestling between boulevard Saint-Germain and boulevard Raspail in the 7ᵗʰ arrondissement, Galerie Clémande presents furniture, lamps and decorative pieces from the 1950s, 1960s and 1970s selected for their special character.

There is also a wide range of jewellery from the great French, Italian and American couturiers (Dior, Chanel, Saint-Laurent...), carefully selected by Rose Marie Burgevin, who has a genuine passion for her creations that she is only too eager to share with her clients.

⁻ 3, rue de Luynes, 75007
Metro: Rue-du-bac

A Tribute to the 21ˢᵗ Century
Galerie May

Tables, chairs, shelves, lamps and mirrors. A chic, yet quirky gallery belonging to the artist Maylis Queyrat and interior designer Charles Tassin which presents tables, chairs, shelves, lamps and mirrors in a *neo-bourgeois* style and seventies-revival glamour.

Apart from its interior design projects, the gallery also produces furniture, adopting contemporary approaches to marquetry, lacquered works and ceramics. The result is minimalist, a marvellous expression of exquisite international decoration.

⁻ 23, rue de Lille, 75007
Tel: 01 42 61 41 40
Metro: Saint-Germain-des-Prés
www.galerie-may.fr

The Design Pulse
¹ Galerie Kreo

A gallery and production laboratory presenting the finest in contemporary design run by two design experts Clémence and Didier Krzentowski.

In this minimalist setting you'll find limited editions by François Bauchet, Ronan & Erwan Bouroullec, Hella Jongerius, Martin Szekely, and Maarten Van Severen as well as lamps from the 1950s to the present day by Achille Castiglioni, Vittorio Viganò, Jacques Biny, and more.

– 31, rue Dauphine, 75006
Tel: 01 53 10 23 00
Metro: Saint-Germain-des-Prés
www.galeriekreo.fr

Contemporary Art
² Galerie Kamel Mennour

Kamel Mennour's secondary interest after photography is the visual arts. In his magnificent gallery designed by the architects Aldric Beckmann and Françoise N'Thépé, he exhibits major works by Daniel Buren, Claude Levêque, Martin Parr, Anish Kapoor and Tadashi Kawamata. More recently there was Pier Paolo Calzolari with a spectacular exhibition of Arte Povera.

One of Paris's leading contemporary art galleries.

– 47, rue Saint-André-des-Arts, 75006
Tel: 01 56 24 03 63
Metro: Saint-Germain-des-Prés
or Saint-Michel
For another address, visit:
www.kamelmennour.com

Architectural Furniture
Galerie Downtown

François Laffanour's Galerie Downtown opened in 1982 and has since become a temple of contemporary furniture, lamps and decoration by architects and designers. The gallery purveys quintessential 20th- and 21st-century furniture: Jean Prouvé, Charlotte Perriand, Pierre Jeanneret, Serge Jouve, and Georges Jouve, among others.

Until only recently, many of the pieces on show were commonplace in thrift stores, student residences and overseas administrations, so you may be surprised to find the prices slightly expensive.

– 18, rue de Seine, 75006
Tel: 01 46 33 82 41
Metro: Mabillon
www.galeriedowntown.com

Artistic Dialogues
Jousse Entreprise

Philippe Jousse is a huge fan of the likes of Jean Prouvé, Charlotte Perriand, Alexandre Noll, Jean Royère, Mathieu Matégot and Serge Mouille. His gallery stages eclectic, monographic exhibitions, presenting the cutting-edge of contemporary design, which give rise to genuine artistic exchange. There are also works by contemporary ceramicists such as Kristin McKirdy and Emmanuel Boos, while Jousse's son Matthias is a devotee of 1970's designers – Maria Pergay, Roger Tallon, and Michel Boyer.

⌐ 18, rue de Seine, 75006
Tel: 01 53 82 13 60
Metro: Saint-Germain-des-Prés
www.jousse-entreprise.com

Icons of Design
[1] Knoll International

Hans Knoll and his wife Florence changed the face of design when they invented their revolutionary furniture concept incorporating design, interior architecture, textiles and graphics.

Created in East Greenville, Pennsylvania in 1938, Knoll went onto become a essential reference in design and the couple worked with internationally renowned architects and designers such as Gae Aulenti, Frank Gehry, Ross Lovegrove, Lise-Anne Couture and Eero Saarinen – creator of the famous Tulip table and chair.

Knoll also reproduced iconic works such as Marcel Breuer's Wassily chair from 1925, and Ludwig Mies van der Rohe's Barcelona armchair from 1930.

⌐ 268, boulevard Saint-Germain, 75007
Tel: 01 44 18 19 99
Metro: Assemblée nationale
www.knoll.com

Fifties Passion
[2] Galerie Pascal Cuisinier

Pascal Cuisinier is a great admirer of highly sought after functional designs and French works from the 1950s and 1960s. Hence you'll find pieces by Pierre Guariche, Pierre Paulin and Geneviève Dangles, lamps designed by Pierre Disderot.

Each year he organizes a superb monographic exhibition, and also exhibits at the major international fairs such as PAD (Paris Art + Design), Design Miami and Design Basel.

⌐ 13, rue de Seine, 75006
Tel: 01 43 54 34 61
Metro: Saint-Germain-des-Prés
www.galeriepascalcuisinier.com

English Elegance
¹ British Gallery
& Scène Antique Galerie

Philippe and Christine Roux's charming British Gallery unveils their passion for all aspects of 18ᵗʰ and 19ᵗʰ century English furniture – bookshelves, desks, seats, dressers, side tables and paintings. You'll also find finely crafted reproductions of Madeleine Castaing's furniture.

The neighboring Scene Antiques Galerie run by their daughters, Aurore Berreri and Véronique Haslund, presents a beautiful selection of engravings, light fittings, stools, curiosities and model boats, and also specializes in lamps and lampshades.

A great favourite of Ladurée.

— 54, rue de l'Université, 75007
Tel: 01 42 60 19 12
Metro: Rue du Bac
www.british-gallery.com

Rare Editions
² Galerie Alexandre Biaggi

In his elegant gallery with pastel tones, the former auctioneer Alexandre Biaggi presents an exceptional choice of American and European late 20ᵗʰ-century neo-classical furniture by renowned designers such as Gio Ponti, André Arbus and Jean-Michel Frank.

Alongside his decoration and treasure hunting talents, Alexandre Biaggi also works as an interior architecture consultant and produces decorative pieces, furniture and lamps by Simone Crestani, Hervé Van der Straeten, Patrick Naggar and Mauro Fabbro.

We especially love his warm welcome and his subtle, poetic approach to his unorthodox collection of refined, chic furniture.

— 14, rue de Seine, 75006
Tel: 01 44 07 34 73
Metro: Saint-Germain-des-Prés
www.alexandrebiaggi.com

Originality
Galerie Douze

Don't expect anything too classical from the Galerie Douze. Instead revel in its collection of 18ᵗʰ-20ᵗʰ century originals: a spectacular wooden, cast-iron, crystal and bronze neo-Gothic chandelier; 19ᵗʰ century pastel works; plaster pieces from the 1940s; a Madeleine Castaing ocelot rug and plaster sculptures – such as the Natacha Natova dancer, by the sculptor Serge Youriévitch, which became the mould for a bronze exhibited at the Petit Palais.

An elegant gallery expressing the refined sensibilities of its owners, Nicolas Sergeeff and Régis Aernouts.

— 12, rue Jacob, 75006
Tel: 06 70 99 94 31
Metro: Saint-Germain-des-Prés

A passion for fusion
[1] India Mahdavi

The boutique of the internationally renowned Iranian architect, designer and scenographer, India Mahdavi offering a hurly-burly fusion of styles and genres zinging with colour, textures, and motifs. India Mahdavi has become a key figure in the design world and is behind some of the city's finest interiors – the Café Français, the Restaurant Germain and the Brasserie Thoumieux; other acclaimed interiors include the Townhouse Hotel in Miami and the Connaught Hotel restaurant in London.

Her boutique offers elegant furniture and home accessories – ceramic coffee cups, embroidered woolen cushions, cashmere blankets from Mongolia, glass lamps from Murano, as well as table decorations by Taher Chemirik, Marie Christophe wire sculptures and Rupert Shrive's crumpled paintings.

– 3 and 19, rue Las Cases, 75007
Tel: 01 45 55 67 67 and 01 45 55 88 88
Metro: Solférino
www.india-mahdavi.com

The Poetry of Opposites
KRD

At KRD, the interior designer Klavs Rosenfalck shares his passion for finely crafted mid-century pieces of furniture from Scandinavia and the Mediterranean: tables, sideboards, display cases, and lamps by Kai Kristiansen, Hans Wegner, Verner Panton, and Vilhelm Kucha among others.

In this world of multifarious styles you'll also find fireplace accessories, tableware, vintage and contemporary pieces, glassware by Orrefors, Kosta Boda, Anna Torfs, textiles, statues, figurines and candlesticks. A delicious combination of Mediterranean warmth and Nordic cool.

– 58, rue de Bourgogne, 75007
Tel: 01 44 18 94 88
Metro: Assemblée nationale
www.krd.fr

Barbarian Baroque
En attendant les barbares

Since 1983, Agnès Kentish has been promoting works by the contemporary designers Garouste & Bonetti, Andrée Putman, Éric Jourdan, Christian Ghion, Arik Lévy, Éric Robin, Éric Schmitt, Mathilde Brétillot and Élisabeth Garouste. There is a predominantly heavy-metal theme with gilt-iron iron and forged iron lamps, ceiling and walls fittings, as well as hand-wrought and beeswax-seasoned iron pedestal and console tables. Baroque elegance with a delectable hint of barbarianism.

– 35, rue de Grenelle, 75007
Tel: 01 42 22 65 25
Metro: Rue du Bac
www.barbares.com

Attractive Classicism

[1] Gilles Dériot

A traditional antiques boutique run by a design expert and fervent promoter of 18th and 19th century furniture and decoration from France and elsewhere. There are rock crystal wall lamps, Renaissance-style furniture, armchairs upholstered in antique tapestries, and mahogany coat stands.

What the boutique lacks in drama and decorative arrangement, the owner makes up for in his passion for antiques.

– Marché Serpette
  110, rue des Rosiers, lane 1, stand 37,
  93400 Saint-Ouen
  Tel: 01 40 12 75 62
  and 06 11 92 27 46
  Metro: Porte de Clignancourt

That 18th-Century Vibe

[2] La Maison du Roy

Stepping inside La Maison du Roy is a trip back in time to 18th century noble boudoirs. The owners Pascale and Carole Lemoine offer precious antiques exuding royalty: 18th century portraits and armchairs, as well as wonders from Italy or Greece such columns and seats, terracotta busts, paintings depicting scenes of chivalry and baroque jewellery.

You'll find the same approach in the couple's other 9th arrondissement gallery 24 passage Jouffroy.

– Marché Serpette
  110, rue des Rosiers, lane 1, stand 37,
  93400 Saint-Ouen
  Tel: 01 40 12 75 62 and 06 11 92 27 46
  Metro: Porte de Clignancourt

Distant Adventures

Le Monde du voyage

Elegant vintage travel accessories by the great names of design: trunks, suitcases, bags and purses by Vuitton, Goyard, Hermès and Chanel, including a beautiful selection of well-preserved Vuitton trunks. Simply running your fingers over the engravings affords a delicious frisson of nostalgia. There are also accessories and collectibles, like a Birkin purse by Hermès, haute-couture jewellery by Chanel or Gripoix, Jaeger-LeCoultre watches and clocks, ashtrays, trinket bowls, etc.

A family business now in the hands by Helen and Alain Zisul, the boutique oozes tales of adventure in faraway lands and features in some of the world's most exclusive guides.

– Marché Serpette
  108-110, rue des Rosiers, lane 3,
  stand 15, 93400 Saint-Ouen
  Tel: 01 40 12 64 03
  Metro: Porte de Clignancourt
  www.lemondeduvoyage.com

Crystal Clear
¹ Philippe Lachaux

The place to find the finest 19th- and 20th-century Murano chandeliers in the whole of Paris. Philippe Lachaux and his Italian partner are seasoned treasure hunters.

Some of his finds decorate Ladurée's tearooms, while others have featured in major national exhibitions such as the 'Masterpieces of Glass, from the Renaissance to the 21st century' exhibition at the Musée Maillol in Paris; that's just how good he is!

His gallery partner Claude Aucouturier meanwhile takes care of their other speciality: antique oak spiral staircases.

- Marché Biron
  85, rue des Rosiers, lane 2,
  stands 156, 157 and 158,
  93400 Saint-Ouen
  Tel: 06 07 49 62 74 and 06 08 23 51 77
  Metro: Porte de Clignancourt
  www.antiquitesphilippelachaux.fr

Fine Lines
² Le 7 Paul Bert

A magnificent boutique specializing in French furniture of the 1950s and pieces by the great names in design: Swedish gilt-brass candlesticks, Joe Colombo armchairs by Kartell, a Warren Platner table by Knoll International, a varnished mahogany Maxime Old buffet from Cuba, and more.

A warm emporium purveying an attractive range of 20th-century decorative art and design.

- Marché Paul Bert
  96-110, rue des Rosiers, lane 7,
  93400 Saint-Ouen
  Tel: 06 85 41 35 89
  Metro: Porte de Clignancourt
  www.le7paulbert.com

Beside the Fire
³ Marc Maison

For the past twenty years, Marc Maison has specialized in antique fireplaces – mantelpieces in wood or marble, cast-iron fire boxes, grates, and stucco mouldings. They also stock everything to surround a fireplace; parquet-floorings, stairs and banisters, wooden panelling and stained-glass windows, as well as garden decorations; such as Medici vases, statues, fountains and benches. Home, after all, is where the hearth is.

- Marché Biron
  120, rue des Rosiers, lane 6,
  stand 83, 93400 Saint-Ouen
  Tel: 06 60 62 61 90
  and 01 42 25 12 79
  (by appointment only)
  Metro: Porte de Clignancourt
  www.marcmaison.fr

Gourmet Antiques

¹Bachelier Antiquités

For thirty years, Françoise-Anne and François Bachelier have specialized in antique kitchen ware and wine accessories, and share their passion for the culinary arts. Their boutique has a traditional country kitchen feel with copper pots and utensils hanging from the shelves and walls. You'll find every accessory, from dressers and porcelain wood-burning stoves, to chopping blocks, cake moulds and poaching pans.

Gastronomy is the Bachelier's philosophy and for the last fifteen years, the couple has held a biennial terrine competition attracting participants from Japan and Australia.

- Marché Paul Bert
  18, rue Paul-Bert, lane 1, stand 17,
  93400 Saint-Ouen
  Tel : 01 40 11 89 98 and 06 19 55 15 38
  Metro: Porte de Clignancourt
  www.bachelier-antiquites.com

20th-Century Fusions

² Antiquités Labergère-Vauban

Rémy Labergère and Vincent Vauban abandoned their passion for the 19th century to turn their attentions to charming 1940s–1970s furniture from Italy, Belgium and France.

Here you'll find oak, cedar, rosewood and mahogany pieces, with some designer creations. There are also ceramics, rattan-framed mirrors, lamps and fittings. A chic collection of catholic influences with a retro-vintage feel.

- Marché Paul Bert
  85, rue des Rosiers, lane 1, stand 142,
  93400 Saint-Ouen
  Tel : 06 84 20 11 37 and 06 84 08 16 07
  Metro: Porte de Clignancourt

The Land of Ceramics

Aidjolate Antiquités

In Franco-Swiss patois, 'Aidjolate' means a 'joy-filled home', and truly, Laurence Vauclair's boutique offers many wonders from historical French artisans to fill your abode with unalloyed bliss.

The owner is an expert in ceramics especially 19th-century barbotines and maiolicas from the prestigious French manufactories, and there are rare pieces by Thomas Victor, who in the 19th century reproduced Bernard Palissy's famous polychrome enamel works.

The store also sells magnificent rattan furniture redolent of the exoticism of late 19th-century winter gardens.

- Marché Paul Bert
  96, rue des Rosiers, lane 6, stand 79,
  93400 Saint-Ouen
  Tel : 06 09 48 27 86
  Metro: Porte de Clignancourt
  www.laurence-vauclair.com

Bouquets from Bygone Days

[1] Odorantes

An off-beat boutique run by the artist-florists Emmanuel Sammartimo and Christophe Hervé, presenting all the charm of the hauntingly poetic gardens of yesteryear.

The black and grey floors, walls and furnishings and provide the perfect setting for the riot of colour within, and seem to intensify the explosive shades of anemones, sweet peas, pom-pom peonies and delicately scented garden roses. The store stocks fresh cut seasonal flowers from small producers close to Paris.

– 9, rue Madame, 75006
Tel: 01 42 84 03 00
Metro: Saint-Germain-des-Prés
www.odorantes-paris.com

Haute Couture Florets

[2] Moulié

At Moulié, *you* choose your bouquet. If the profusion of blooms bewilders you, the florists are on hand to help you create a flower selection to suit your budget. Look out for its magnificent Meilland and Jeanne Moreau roses; its orchids are the finest in Paris.

Moulié is also the official supplier to embassies, ministries and gala events in the worlds of fashion and art.

– 8, place du Palais-Bourbon, 75007
Tel: 01 45 51 78 43
Metro: Assemblée nationale
www.mouliefleurs.com

Cottage Garden

[3] L'Art en fleurs

A traditional village store front with cottage feel containing a floral Eden in the heart of the Paris. Natacha Heurtematte specializes in floral decoration for events and arranges bouquets of unconventional combinations of blooms in glass jars.

There are traditional roses, hydrangeas, Mexican marigolds, wallflowers, and freesias as well as magnificent orchid compositions.

– 38, rue de Varenne, 75007
Tel: 01 53 71 98 29
Metro: Sèvres-Babylone

Flowers In-Season

Rosa Luna

No garish blooms to be found here, only ethereal compositions. Opened in 2009, Rosa Luna specializes in seasonal flowers, grown exclusively in France.

Its florist-owners Olivier, Frederic and Rena, met at college and share the same passion for nature's beauty. The boutique is sensitively decorated to showcase the floral stars of the show in all their glory.

– 24, boulevard Raspail, 75007
Tel: 01 42 22 00 22
Metro: Rue du Bac

Culture

{ Culture }

Paris is the capital of the Arts. Whether it's painting, sculpture, religious art, graphics, archeology, fashion, or literature that appeals to you, Paris has it all. The city is crammed with a multitude of museums – major state institutions in vast palatial settings and smaller heritage museums in magnificent mansions. There are also prestigious foundations and cultural institutions – protectors of the world's cultural wonders. These monuments to civilization often have enchanting grounds that are perfect for relaxing, strolling or reading in. And because literature is essential to art, and how we perceive it, we have also added a handful of Paris's plethora of delightful bookstores.

Paris has some of the world's greatest and grandest museums – not only do they house iconic works, but their magnificent buildings are works of art in their own right, housing treasures as diverse as the Mona Lisa, Jeanne Lanvin's bathroom, Cézanne's Montagne Sainte-Victoire and Elsa Schiaparelli dresses.

··· THE LOUVRE MUSEUM ···

The Louvre's early foundations date back to the 12th century when it was a fortified castle. Over the centuries, it was rebuilt and transformed into a royal residence. Visiting the whole of the Louvre to view each and every one of its myriad masterpieces – paintings, sculptures, Islamic arts, and Eastern, Etruscan, Greek and Roman antiquities – is an undertaking that could take several weeks even with a guide familiar with its maze of galleries, and you'd definitely need a robust pair of comfortable shoes. One approach is to choose a different theme each day. Why not start with Napoleon III's ceremonial apartments in the rue de Rivoli wing? Don't miss the new galleries, dedicated to 12th, 18th and 19th century French art objects, decorated by Jacques Garcia on the second floor of the Sully wing.

⁻ **Palais du Louvre, 75001** 🔑 **Tel : 01 40 20 50 50 or 01 40 20 53 17**
🔑 **Metro: Palais-Royal or Musée du Louvre** 🔑 **www.louvre.fr**

··· MUSÉE DES ARTS DECORATIFS ···

The Museum of Decorative Arts is housed in the Rohan and Marsan wings of the Louvre. Created in 1882 it was designed in the spirit of 19th-century Universal Exhibitions. Overlooking the Tuileries Garden and Carrousel, the museum stages regular theme-based exhibitions and houses a variety of collections – French decorative arts (enamels, lacquer work, glass, ceramics, and papier-maché Napoleon III furniture) as well as design, fashion and textiles, commercial art, graphic design, photography, jewellery and toys, encompassing all periods from the Middle Ages to the present day – Renaissance, 17th-19th centuries, Art Nouveau and Art Deco. Of special note: the couturier Jeanne Lanvin's private apartment created in 1924 by Armand Albert Rateau, and the superb bookstore on the ground floor.

⁻ **107, rue de Rivoli, 75001** 🔑 **Tel : 01 44 55 57 50**
🔑 **Metro: Palais-Royal or Musée du Louvre** 🔑 **www.lesartsdecoratifs.fr**

... PALAIS GALLIERA,
MUSÉE DE LA MODE DE LA VILLE DE PARIS ...

Paris's fashion museum is housed in the neo-Renaissance-style Galleria Palace built by Paul René Léon Ginain in 1879 to house the Duchess de Galliera's art collections, which were finally transferred to the Palazzo Rosso in Genoa. The current museum opened in 1977 and shares its director, Olivier Saillard's, passion for clothing and fashion accessories. Some clothing and accessories are so fragile and rare that they are often only exhibited on a temporary basis. The lay-out is uncluttered giving pride of place to the exquisite garments. After the visit take a stroll in the museum's garden.

− 10, avenue Pierre Ier-de-Serbie, 75116   Tel: 01 56 52 86 00   Metro: Iéna
  www.palaisgalliera.paris.fr

... MUSÉE D'ORSAY ...

Proudly perched on the banks of the Seine facing the Tuileries, this former train station designed by Victor Laloux for the 1900 Universal Exhibition today houses some of the major works of the second half of the 19th century. After a period of disuse, the station became a listed historical monument in 1978 and was transformed into a museum which opened in 1986. The museum's spectacular architecture is the work of the Italian Gae Aulenti, and houses paintings, sculptures, furniture, decorative arts, graphics, photography and architecture. The museum's major appeal is its comprehensive collection of impressionist paintings; the Art Nouveau furniture and sculptures are also popular. On the top floor is the Cafe des Hauteurs offering one of the finest views of Paris, while the museum's restaurant is located in the station hotel's former dining room.

− 1, rue de la Légion-d'honneur, 75007   Tel: 01 40 49 48 14   Metro: Solférino
and RER C Musée d'Orsay   www.musee-orsay.fr

A Garden of Paris

¹ Musée de la Vie romantique

The museum is housed in a delightful mansion typical of the Bourbon Restoration. This gorgeous residence comprises two floors, a garden courtyard with stunning trellised wisteria, and two workshop-outhouses. During the 1830s, its owner, the Dutch-born portrait painter, Ary Scheffer, played host to a series of key figures of the arts and literature such as George Sand, Chopin, Liszt, Delacroix and Rossini.

The building was recently redecorated by Jacques Garcia and currently stages two exhibitions per year. On the first floor is correspondence from the 19th century novelist George Sand, portraits, furniture and jewellery from the 17th and 19th centuries. On the second floor are canvases by Ary Scheffer and the artists he patronized.

— 16, rue Chaptal, 75009
Tel: 01 55 31 95 67
Metro: Saint-Georges

18th-Century Glory

² Musée Cognac-Jay

A minuscule yet magnificent museum in the heart of the Marais set in a listed 16th century mansion, specializing in 17th and 18th century art: there is a superb Rembrandt, paintings by Canaletto, Tiepolo and Boucher, sculptures by Houdon and Lemoyne, Saxony porcelain, furniture by Carlin, Oeben and Jacob, miniatures, and more.

The collection once belonged to Ernest Cognacq, founder of Paris's grand department store La Samaritaine, and his wife, Marie-Louise Jay, and was bequeathed to the City of Paris in 1928.

— 8, rue Elvézir, 75003
Tel: 01 40 27 07 21
Metro: Saint-Paul or Chemin-Vert
www.museecognacqjay.paris.fr

The Art of Personal Effects

Musée Delacroix

A small museum dedicated to the life and work of the 19th-century French artist, Eugene Delacroix. The building, a listed monument, is enchanting – from the porch, a staircase leads to an apartment overlooking a charming garden invisible from the street – and it is no surprise that Delacroix chose to live here until his death in 1863.

Today the museum is part of the Louvre Museum and houses masterpieces such as *Mary Magdalena in the Wilderness and Education of the Virgin*, as well the artist's drawings and personal effects. A moving, enriching experience.

— 6, rue de Furstenberg, 75006
Tel: 01 44 41 86 50
Metro: Saint-Germain-des-Prés or Mabillon
www.musee-delacroix.fr

The Heart of Sculpture

1 Musée Rodin

Not far from Les Invalides is the Hotel Biron built in the 18th century by the architect Jean Aubert. Here the sculptor Auguste Rodin once lived and today the museum houses many of his famous works as well drawings, photographs and the sculptor's personal art collection; there is also a room dedicated to the work of Camille Claudel.

The enchanting grounds with their cafe and rose garden make for an exquisitely relaxing experience away from the hustle and bustle of the city. Here you'll also discover some of the sculptor's masterpieces like *The Thinker, The Burgers of Calais* and *The Gates of Hell*, as well as a cafe.

⌐ 79, rue de Varenne, 75007
Tel: 01 44 198 61 10
Metro: Varenne or Invalides
www.musee-rodin.fr

Private Collections

2 Musée Picasso

Paris's shrine to the pioneering 20th century artist Pablo Picasso. The museum, set in an 18th-century mansion, first opened in 1985 was recently renovated in 2014. The building contains many of Picasso's major works as well as the artist's archives of drawings, sketches, ceramics, sculptures, sketch books, engravings and photographs.

There is also Picasso's personal collection including paintings by Le Nain, Corot, Vuillard, Cézanne, Gauguin, among others and furniture by Diego Giacometti. You can also visit Picasso's private garden.

⌐ 5, rue de Thorigny, 75003
Tel: 01 85 56 00 36
Metro: Saint-Paul,
Saint-Sébastien-Froissard
or Chemin-Vert
www.museepicassoparis.fr

Contemporary Art

La Maison Rouge

Not far from La Bastille, La Maison Rouge is a contemporary art foundation which stages some of Paris most unusual and fascinating artistic events, including several monographic exhibitions per year.

Set in an abandoned factory, a vast space covering several floors, La Maison Rouge was created by Antoine de Galbert, a contemporary art collector renowned for his fresh approach to painting, sculpture and video.

La Maison Rouge also has a branch of the famous organic English-style cafe, Rose Bakery, which is totally redesigned several times a year, by the scenographer Émilie Bonaventure, to match the theme of the current exhibition. Not something you find everywhere!

⌐ 10, boulevard de la Bastille, 75012
Tel: 01 40 01 08 81
Metro: Quai de la Rapée
www.lamaisonrouge.org

Convent Culture

¹ Musée Zadkine

Not far from the Luxembourg Garden, Le Musée Zadkine is one of the rare surviving workshop-museums that bear testimony to the Montparnasse of the 1920s, when the district was the heart of Parisian intellectual and literary life.

Housed in a former outbuilding of the Notre Dame de Sion convent, the museum is an enchanting space bathed in natural light, which was recently renovated to recreate an early-20th century workshop atmosphere.

It was here that the Russian sculptor Ossip Zadkine and his wife, the artist Valentine Prax, lived from 1928 to 1967. The museum exhibits seventy of Zadkine's sculptures in a variety of media and its garden contains the couple's favourite plants and flowers.

– 100 bis, rue d'Assas, 75006
Tel: 01 55 42 77 20
Metro: Vavin
www.zadkine.paris.fr

Personal Collections

² Le musée Maillol

In 1995, the sculptor Aristide Maillol's muse and model, Dina Vierny, created the Dina Vierny Foundation to protect the artist's own work and personal collections. Behind its magnificent fountain façade sculpted by the 18th-century artist Edeme Bouchardon, the museum stages regular exhibitions, such as their recent major exhibitions focusing on art in the age of the Medicis and the Borgias. The top floor is devoted to the museum's permanent collections of 20th-century paintings, sculptures and drawings.

– 59-61, rue de Grenelle, 75007
Tel: 01 42 22 59 58
Metro: Rue du Bac
www.museemaillol.com

Orchids and Beehives

Musée du Luxembourg

Renovated in 2012 by two stars of world architecture, Shigeru Ban and Jean de Gastines, the Musée du Luxembourg stages regular exhibitions of paintings from the Renaissance to the 20th century on themes as diverse as the Tudors and 'Fragonard in Love'. The museum is set in the enchanting Luxembourg Garden created in 1612 for Marie de Medicis.

Apart from the lawns, tree-lined promenades and flowerbeds, you'll find the Medici fountain depicting Polyphemus discovering the lovers Acis and Galatea, an orange grove, oleanders galore, an orchard, greenhouses with tropical orchids and beehives. A delightful haven of calm.

– 19, rue de Vaugirard, 75006
Tel: 01 40 13 62 00
Metro: Odéon or Saint-Sulpice,
RER B Luxembourg
www.museeduluxembourg.fr

18th Century Style
Musée
Nissim de Camondo

In 1911, the wealthy banker Count Moïse de Camondo entrusted the architect René Sergent with building a home for his decorative arts collections on the edge of the Parc Monceau. The result? One of Paris's most attractive residences.

Camondo's furnishings and 18th century western and far-eastern art objects, paintings and sculptures are presented as though in a private home maintained in its original condition.

The kitchen with its rotisserie and grand central stove is spectacular and the servants' dining room offers a glimpse of mansion life of a bygone era.

— 63, rue de Monceau, 75008
Tel: 01 53 89 06 40
Metro: Monceau or Villiers
www.lesartsdecoratifs.fr/francais/
nissim-de-camondo

Home to the Past
¹ Musée
Jacquemart-André

Édouard André, the heir to a Protestant banking family, and his wife, the artist Nélie Jacquemart devoted their lives to art. This divine palace, built by the architect Henri Parent and completed in 1875, became home to their impressive collections. The couple had a passion for 18th century painting, French decorative arts and Gobelins tapestries.

Once the setting for fêted high-society gatherings and lavish balls, today the mansion is a heritage home and museum with a sumptuous dining room, Second Empire music room, sculpture gallery, winter garden and a series of apartments exhibiting works by Chardin, Canaletto and Nattier.

— 158, boulevard Haussmann, 75008
Tel: 01 45 62 11 59
Metro: Miromesnil
www.musee-jacquemart-andre.com

Museum cafes

Paris's museum-gardens often have delightful cafes, offering the perfect pause while perusing masterpieces. There is **Le Jardin du Petit Palais cafe**, decorated with neo-classical mosaics and colonnades; **Les Ombres**, on the roof of the Musée Quai Branly, affording one of the finest views of Paris; the **Musée d'Orsay's restaurant** with its 1900s décor created by Gabriel Ferrier and Benjamin Constant; the **Musée Rodin cafe** terrace overlooking a French garden and Rodin's sculptures; and the **Cafe Jacquemard-André**, in the former dining of the eponymous museum (see above).

The Avant-Garde

¹ Fondation Cartier

Opened in 1984, the Fondation Cartier is Paris's avant-garde showcase for contemporary creation, whether photography, installations, video, sculpture or paintings. The foundation also stages concerts and dance performances, and its 'nomad nights' are legendary. It has a reputation for exhibiting the hidden face of art – young artists' creations and established artist's more obscure and personal works.

The building, a magnificent glass and metal-framed structure designed by the French architect Jean Nouvel, is set in attractive grounds – a verdant haven of peace in the heart of Paris.

— 261, boulevard Raspail, 75014
Tel: 01 42 18 56 50
Metro: Raspail
www.fondation.cartier.com

The Home of Photography

² Fondation Cartier-Bresson

Not far from Montparnassse, the Fondation Cartier-Bresson is naturally home to the work of the French photographer Henri Cartier-Bresson, but also stages exhibitions of the world's finest shutterbugs. The museum is a fascinating radiant workshop-style space with a listed glass-ceiling.

Inside you'll find original prints, as well as proof sheets, drawings, publications, rare books, films and posters.

The Foundation stages three major exhibitions per year, as well as video projections and bi-monthly conferences organized by the art critic and novelist Natacha Wolinski. A moving tribute to the art and its heritage in an age where the digital reigns.

— 2, impasse Lebouis, 75014
Tel: 01 56 80 27 00
Metro: Gaîté
www.henricartierbresson.org

The Best of Haute Couture

³ Fondation Pierre Bergé– Yves Saint Laurent

The Fondation Pierre Bergé–Yves Saint Laurent was created in 2002, when Yves Saint Laurent went into retirement. Dedicated to the conservation and promotion of the couturier's magnificent heritage, the Foundation is home to five thousand haute-couture garments, fifteen-thousand accessories, fifty-thousand sketches and drawings, as well as press cuttings, photos and videos paying tribute to YSL's genius.

As consummate patrons to the arts, Yves Saint Laurent and Pierre Bergé also provided exhibition spaces for others.

— 5, avenue Marceau, 75116
Tel: 01 44 31 64 00
Metro: Alma-Marceau
www.fondation-pb-ysl.net

A Spectacle of Nature

[1] Espace culturel Louis Vuitton

On the eighth floor of Louis Vuitton's spectacular flagship store on the Champs Elysees, you'll find its art museum and cultural centre commanding a magnificent view of the Champs Elysees and Paris.

The centre is now an annex for the Foundation Louis Vuitton, whose HQ, also a showcase for contemporary art and photography, is housed in a spectacular curvaceous-glass Frank Gehry creation set in the verdant surroundings of the Bois de Boulogne.

The Foundation (8 avenue du Mahatma Gandhi, 75116; metro: Les Sablons), like the Champs-Elysées cultural centre, stages art exhibitions, conferences and performances.

— **60, rue Bassano, 75008**
Tel: 01 53 57 52 03 or 01 40 69 96 00
Metro: George V
www.louisvuitton-espaceculturel.com
and www.fondationlouisvuitton.fr/en/

Japanese Culture

[2] Maison de la Culture du Japon à Paris

The Japanese cultural centre in Paris contains everything the Land of the Rising Sun has to offer. There are naturally exhibitions, projections and performances of Japanese art, film, dance and music, but also conferences and classes in Japanese rituals, cookery, calligraphy, language, literature, *ikebana* floral art and origami.

Designed by the Anglo-Japanese architectural duo Masayuki Yamanaka and Kenneth Armstrong, this ambitious glass-fronted architectural project is home to both the cultural centre and the Japan Foundation in France.

Its eleven stories contain boutiques, exhibition rooms, tea pavilions, cooking spaces, classrooms and a library. The essence of Japan in microcosm.

— **101 bis, quai Branly, 75007**
Tel: 01 44 37 95 01
Metro: Bir-Hakeim
www.mcjp.fr

Haute Couture Publications
7L

The couturier Karl Lagerfeld opened his own bookstore to share his passion for imagery, paper and words. Here he presents everything he loves in published form: the decorative arts, art and contemporary art, design, photography, poetry and illustrated works from small publishers dating from 1900 to 1930. Paradoxically, you'll find little literature devoted to fashion.

- 7, rue de Lille, 75007
  Tel: 01 42 92 03 58
  Metro: Saint-Germain-des-Prés
  www.librairie7l.com

Literary Workshop
La Chambre claire

A bookstore that is a must-see for collectors, photographers, cinema buffs, and lovers of rare publications and the latest art books.
La Chambre Claire also stages art exhibitions and regular book-signings.

- 14, rue Saint-Sulpice, 75006
  Tel: 01 46 34 04 31
  Metro: Odéon
  www.la-chambre-claire.fr

Literally British
[1] Galignani

The most famous English bookstore in Paris which has been nestling in rue de Rivoli's arcades since 1801. Everything a well-stocked comprehensive store should contain: the latest novels, best-sellers and travel guides, as well as politics, economics, history, the arts, interior design, photography, cookery, etc. This spacious, calm and eminently browsable store is a haven for bookworm ex-pats and tourists; there are also French and foreign language sections.

- 224, rue de Rivoli, 75001
  Tel: 01 42 60 76 07
  Metro: Tuileries
  www.galignani.com

The Soul of the District
[2] Librairie Delamain

Founded in 1700, it is considered to be Paris's oldest bookstore and was once home to Paris's leading literary figures such as Jean Cocteau, Colette and Louis Aragon.
The store stocks everything from literature and thrillers, to the humanities and the arts, and its antique ,ceiling-high solid-oak shelves are crammed with contemporary literature and hallowed leather-bound 18th-century tomes.

- 155, rue Saint-Honoré, 75001
  Tel: 01 42 61 48 78
  Metro: Palais Royal-Musée du Louvre
  www.librairie-delamain.com

THE FIRST

ENGLISH BOOKSHOP

ESTABLISHED

ON THE

CONTINENT

The Soul of Saint Germain des Prés

¹ L'Écume des pages

A traditional browsing-hole replete with French and foreign literature, poetry, travel chronicles, arts, history, psychoanalysis and the complete works of the greats.

Apart from its delightfully recherché selection, the store offers two major bonuses: firstly that it sells Ladurée books and stationery; and secondly that it is open until midnight every weekday and until 10pm on Sundays.

— 174, boulevard Saint-Germain, 75006
Tel: 01 45 48 54 48
Metro: Saint-Germain-des-Prés
www.ecumedespages.com

So chic

² Librairie Assouline

An elegant bookstore containing magnificent and often expensive works focusing on fashion, decoration, architecture and cinema, published exclusively by the bookstore. It also has an elegant salon with leather armchairs, artwork and a stationery corner, purveying silk ribbons and wax seals.

— 35, rue Bonaparte, 75006
Tel: 01 43 29 23 20
Metro: Saint-Germain-des-Prés
For another address, visit:
www.assouline.com

Accessible Art Books

Taschen

The beautiful Paris bookstore belonging to the renowned German art publisher Taschen, founded in Cologne in 1980. The store sells art and architecture books, comic books and city guides at very reasonable prices.

In Taschen's works, art, photography and illustrations are given pride of place, accompanied by short texts in English, German and French.

— 2, rue de Buci, 75006
Tel: 01 40 51 79 22
Metro: Saint-Germain-des-Prés
www.taschen.com

Young at heart

Chantelivre

A home to children's literature, stocking the finest in illustrated books, traditional tales, comic books, pop-up books and much much more besides.

The bookstore caters for all ages, and moms and dads will also find the latest novels, attractive art books and guides.

One of Paris's finest bookstores, not far from the Bon Marché department store.

— 13, rue de Sèvres, 75006
Tel: 01 45 48 87 90
Metro: Sèvres-Babylone
www.chantelivre.com

Ladurée in Paris

On rue Royale, avenue des Champs-Elysées and rue Bonaparte, you'll find the quintessential magic of Ladurée in Paris ...

··· LADURÉE ROYALE ···

Opened in 1862, Ladurée Royale is our flagship eatery and pioneer store. Its chic interior exudes a warm glow. The second floor has been completely renovated but the wooden panelled first floor has been delicately restored to preserve the original emblematic frescoes of gourmet muses and cherubic bakers in all their glory. Our world-renowned seasonal menu offers simple flavoursome fare. For the main-course, look out for the Ladurée omelet or the chicken vol-au-vent with wild mushrooms. For dessert, you'll naturally find the finest macaroons in Paris, as well as croissants crammed with walnuts, and a wide range of France's finest traditional *patisseries*.

— 16, rue Royale, 75008   Tel: 01 42 60 21 79   Metro: Madeleine

··· LADURÉE CHAMPS-ÉLYSÉES ···

Opened in September 1997, Ladurée Champs-Élysées is our flagship store. The brainchild of Ladurée's CEO, David Holder, and his father Francis Holder, founder of the Holder group, designed by the master of French *art de vivre*, Jacques Garcia, this unique eatery shares the refinement of our rue Royale emporium. On the first floor, the Eiffel-style glass ceiling and terrace look out onto the beautiful bustling avenue. On the rue Lincoln side is the Le Bar Ladurée (see p.18), with a lunch menu that is different to that of the tearoom, and that serves macaroon cocktails all day as well as a wide variety of aperitifs and after-dinner liqueurs; it is especially popular in the evening. The second-floor is composed of a succession of rooms, each with its own special atmosphere, dedicated to three 19th-century society women and patrons of the arts; La Paëva, the Countess of Castiglione, and Mathilde Bonaparte. There is also a chocolate store and library. The tearoom is open every day from 7.30am to midnight, serving breakfast, lunch, tea and dinner. Of special note: the Champs-Elysées Club Sandwich and the Concorde Salad with chicken and spinach shoots at lunch, and for dessert the Raspberry Rose *Saint Honoré* or the rose *religieuse*.

— 75, avenue des Champs-Elysées, 75008   Tel: 01 40 75 08 75
  Metro: Franklin Delano Roosevelt or Metro: George V

⸙ Ladurée Bonaparte ⸙

Tucked away in the heart of Saint Germain des Prés, you'll find our third tearoom. This enticing emporium to gourmet delights is also a tribute to elegance and tradition. Its two levels were designed by Roxane Rodriguez in the style of the decorator Madeleine Castaing the former occupant of the apartments, so the décor is deliberately homely and comfortable. The first floor has a *macaron* boutique and tea-room bedecked in panoramic-print wallpaper while soothing 'blue room' on the second floor is decorated with old photographs. The menu is delectably festive with delicious club sandwiches and warm French bread served with maple syrup, jam or Chantilly cream.

— 21, rue Bonaparte, 75006   Tel: 01 44 07 64 87   Metro: Saint-Germain-des-Prés

You'll also find Ladurée restaurants and sales outlets at the Printemps Haussmann, in Orly Ouest and Roissy Charles-de-Gaulle airports and Versailles.

— www.laduree.com

Contents

Culture

PHOTOGRAPHY CREDITS
All photographs by Pierre-Olivier Signe, with the exception of:
p. 27 La Grande Épicerie: upper left © DR – upper right © Virgile Guinard
p. 51 Carven: © Carven
p. 63 Louboutin: © Louboutin
p. 64 La Droguerie: top © Suzie Laguilhaumie
p. 95 Declercq Passementiers: top © Declercq Passementiers
p. 95 Houlès: below © Houlès
p. 96 Atelier Prométhée: top © Atelier Prométhée
p 103 Galerie Yves Gastou: top © Luxproduction.com
p. 104 Galerie Kamel Mennour: top right and below left © View of the exhibition: 'Valentin Carron, the Sunshine Motorway at Midnight', 2015
p. 107 Galerie Pascal Cuisinier: top © Galerie Pascal Cuisinier
p. 108 Galerie Alexandre Biaggi: below © Galerie A. Biaggi
p. 111 India Mahdavi: © Thomas Humery courtesy India Mahdavi

p. 125 Musée de la Vie Romantique: top © D. Messina/Musée de la Vie Romantique/Paris Musée
p. 126 Musée Picasso: below left © Béatrice Hatala for the Musée National Picasso-Paris, 2014
p. 126 Musée Rodin: top and below left © Musée Rodin/Jérôme Manoukian
p. 129 Musée Maillol: below left © Philippe Abergel – below right © Aristide Maillol, *Dina à la robe rouge*, 1940
p. 130 Musée Jacquemart André: top and below right © C. Recoura – below left © Jean Grisoni
p. 133 Fondation Pierre Bergé-Yves Saint Laurent: Yves Saint Laurent, Georges Braque tribute dress, haute couture collection spring-summer 1988 © Fondation Pierre Bergé -Yves Saint Laurent photo: Alexandre Guirkinger

The photographs on pages 6, 42 74 and 120 showing Le Grand Véfour, Dépôt Vente Luxe, Nobilis and Le Louvre/Grande Pyramide du Louvre were taken by Pierre-Olivier Signe.

First published in the English language in 2016 by VENDOME SCRIPTUM an imprint of

THE VENDOME PRESS
Studio 311
174 Bogart Street
Brooklyn, NY 11206
www.vendomepress.com

CO & BEAR PRODUCTIONS (UK) LTD
63 Edith Grove
London,
UK, SW10 0LB
www.scriptumeditions.co.uk

Publishers: Beatrice Vincenzini, Mark Magowan & Francesco Venturi

Translation © Co & Bear Productions (UK) Ltd, 2016
First published in French by Editions du Chêne –Hachette Livre, 2015
© Éditions du Chêne – Hachette Livre, 2015, for the original work
Translation : Jonno Slysa
Proofreader: James Geist
Graphic design: Marie-Paule Jaulme
English layout: Emilie Serralta
Editorial Manager: Valérie Tognali

Distributed in North America by Abrams Books
Distributed in the rest of world by Thames & Hudson

ISBN: 978-1-902686-86-8
Library of Congress Cataloging-in-Publication Data available upon request.

First Edition
10 9 8 7 6 5 4 3 2 1
Printed in Spain